Living Biblically

Living Biblically

Ten Guides for Fulfillment and Happiness

KALMAN J. KAPLAN

Foreword by Paul Cantz

WIPF & STOCK · Eugene, Oregon

Wipf & Stock
An Imprint of Wipf and Stock Publishers
199 W. 8th Ave., Suite 3
Eugene, OR 97401

www.wipfandstock.com

ISBN 13: 978-1-62032-175-1

Manufactured in the U.S.A.

This book is dedicated to the generations of my family, past, present and future who know how to live biblically, from generation to generation (*mi dor la dor*), embracing the future, rather than fearing it. And to Erich Wellisch, who had the courage to pioneer the emerging and long-overdue field of Biblical Psychology.

Contents

Foreword

FIVE YEARS AGO, WHILE completing the tail-end of my graduate studies, I had the good fortune of coming across one of Professor Kalman Kaplan's essays on biblical psychology. Having been steeped in the psychology and religion literature during the course of writing my dissertation, I frankly did not entertain high expectations from this short, rather obscure article that was casually passed-along to me by my chair. As I read (and re-read) his paper, I came to the realization that Professor Kaplan's scholarship was of a much deeper quality than that to which I had previously been exposed. Rather than studying the behavioral responses to religious phenomenon, as many experimental psychologists tended to do, or retrofitting religious teachings to sync with the latest psychological theories, which has been fairly common practice among pastoral counselors and religious clinicians alike, Professor Kaplan struck at the jugular of modern psychology, so to speak, by questioning the Greek premise on which it was founded and challenging the reader with the simple yet profound question: Why not the Hebrew Bible?!

As a religious individual as well as an aspiring clinical psychologist I had likewise fallen into the unfortunate trap of artificially and arbitrarily segregating biblical wisdom and traditions from psychological theories and practice, as if they represented mutually exclusive enterprises whose integration must be avoided at all costs in order to maintain credibility in both one's religious and professional communities, respectively. This reason/revelation dichotomy that I had internalized was shaken to the core by Professor Kaplan's ideas, and I was intent on meeting this modern David who dared confront the Western psychiatric Goliath with nothing more than a Bible and a pen as his weapon of choice (in addition of course to his vast academic acumen and applied experience in social, developmental, and clinical psychology). At the bottom of the journal article, as is common, I located the author's contact information and, after a rather dramatic "double-take," I realized that Professor Kaplan and I resided in the same condominium building! Had I not already believed in God then this happy coincidence surely would have sparked a conversion experience. Suffice it to say, it was not too long after this time that I introduced myself and thus began the most thrilling intellectual adventure of my life—an intellectual adventure, I must say, that only rivals in quality to my friendship and collegiality with Professor "Kal" Kaplan—a man who truly embodies the biblical worldview in his every thought and action.

But what does it mean to live biblically? The answer, of course, depends in large part to whom the question is posed. To the Orthodox Jew, for instance, living biblically involves orienting one's attitudes and behaviors around the 613 commandments enumerated in the Bible along with the myriad of rabbinic statutes. For the Catholic, living biblically represents adherence to a doctrinal system codified by the Vatican. To the Protestant, the Bible represents the supreme source of authority and promotes living a life consistent with the Gospel. To Professor Kaplan, however, the prospect of living biblically transcends theological divisions and sectarian denominationalism and manifests as more of a holistic worldview: a set of principles and psychological paradigms that are equally as relevant to the nonbeliever as much as to the true believer.

We find ourselves living in an age where most refrain from seeking answers to some of life's most important questions—not because these answers are unobtainable, but rather because the questions have been forgotten. Contrary to what Bertrand Russell and other modern philosophers maintain, the most treasured source of wisdom in the west is not to be found in the dialogues of Plato or the philosophy of Aristotle, but instead resides in the Book of Books: the Hebrew Bible. Western society has been existentially and psychologically anesthetized by the numbing narcotic of scientific positivism and academic correctness so that we believe most of the important questions have already been answered or, even worse, rendered atavistic. Western thinkers have by and large been unwittingly blinded to the timeless wisdom that saturates the Bible.

Since the Enlightenment swept through mid-seventeenth-century Europe, the modern (and now post-modern) intelligentsia has come to privilege the cold, sterile, and ultimately impersonal ethos of scientific empiricism, subsequently promoting this epoch in human history as the so-called "Age of Reason." This was, of course, a shot across the bow to wisdom and knowledge conventionally believed to be derived from "revelatory" sources, chiefly the Bible. As a direct consequence, the biblical worldview has all but been banished from the departments of humanities, philosophy, political science, and most certainly psychology, in the vast majority of universities. The Bible, as if ironically bearing the "mark of Cain," has been relegated to the hinterlands of academic inquiry, reserved on ice for those "superstitious simpletons" who grace the darkened halls of divinity schools and religious seminaries. Nothing less than an academic caste system has been established under the guise of scientific empiricism and progressiveness that has prejudiced generations of thinkers into believing that the Bible has nothing meaningful to contribute to the human quest to live a meaningful and satisfying life.

Although it has been customary to attribute the Age of the Enlightenment to the work of Spinoza, Bayle, Newton, Locke, Voltaire, Rousseau, Montesquieu, Kant, among others, Professor Kaplan's work primarily focuses on contrasting biblical narratives and ethos against the foundational Greek myths, philosophies, and values that anticipated and, in large measure, continue to underwrite much of the contemporary Western worldview. The ancient Greek poems and later dramas are inundated with conflict and tragedy and framed by a pervasive sense of fatalism and hopelessness. Whereas the Ancient Greeks created a quite brilliant and exciting mythopoeia, it was limited in the sense that it highlighted the seedy underbelly of the human condition but completely was bereft of any vision for human redemption. Woefully constrained by a metaphysical landscape that was populated by capricious gods, cryptic oracles, and pre-determined conclusions, the only escape was a misguided, perverted view of freedom found in taking one's own life, i.e., suiciding.

The Bible, in stark contradistinction, presents an intrinsically hopeful and life-affirming message that resonates with the positive and aspirational qualities of the human condition. The loving, firmly covenantal link between humankind and the biblical God established a worldview founded on trust and relational reciprocity. In the economy of biblical metaphysics, freedom isn't to be found by escaping into death, but rather is located within the context of how best to live life as well as in the relational matrix between man and his fellow man and his Creator. Biblical freedom denotes a movement towards a healthy attachment bond rather than an escape from a pathologically enmeshed relationship.

Despite Voltaire's audacious prophesy that within a generation of his passing the Bible would be stricken from Earth, the Bible's relevance as a vibrant source of wisdom and knowledge endures and it remains well-positioned to continue shaping the evolving landscape of the modern world. By de-situating biblical narratives from their theological context, Professor Kaplan has put his finger on the pulse of a never before articulated "biblical logic" and has endeavored to share his findings with the world in the service of shifting the psychiatric zeitgeist from its Ancient Greek foundations to a more robust and positive biblical psychology. *Living Biblically* represents the leading-edge of this ambitious undertaking, and I am confident that you, dear reader, will find this book of supreme value as you strive to live a life of fulfillment and happiness.

Paul Cantz, PsyD
Clinical Assistant Professor
Coordinator, Program of Religion, Spirituality & Mental Health
Department of Psychiatry
University of Illinois at Chicago College of Medicine

Preface

I WOULD LIKE TO acknowledge my indebtedness to the Fulbright International Exchange of Scholars Program and later the John Templeton Foundation for graciously providing funds to develop the ideas for this work, both in America and in Israel. Particular people I would like to thank include Neal Sherman and Judy Stavsky of the Fulbright International Exchange Office in Tel Aviv, Israel; Shlomo Shoham, Amiram Raviv, Danny Algom, and Giora Kienan at Tel Aviv University, as well as my many enthusiastic students at Tel Aviv University and Bar-Ilan University, including in particular, Tal Mandelbaum, Tsachi Galatzer, and Sahar Dolev-Blitental. I would also like to thank Paul Wason and Drew-Rick Miller of the John Templeton Foundation for being of invaluable support in the building of the online course implementing some of this work. My friends Woodrow Kroll, Arnie Cole, and Pam Ovwigho at the Center for Biblical Engagement have been a great source of support and friendship, past, present, and future, including helping to develop, along with the Fulbright Foundation, a Hebrew-language subtitling of the online course. Thanks are also due in this regard to Elizabeth Jones and Paul Cantz, who have helped me administer the course. And to Anand Kumar, Chair of the Psychiatry Department at the University of Illinois College of Medicine, and Dean Bell, Dean at Spertus Institute of Jewish Studies in Chicago, who are now co-hosting the course. And I cannot leave out my friends at ACTS (the Association of Chicago Theological Schools) who have sent our program many students.

My work has depended so deeply on Matthew Schwartz, my coauthor on so many projects contrasting Israel and Hellas. Moriah Markus-Kaplan has been a great source of support for me in these ideas, not always agreeing but always helping to illuminate the underlying issues. She has been far more a *Chava* than an *Antigone* in this regard. Finally, I want to express my indebtedness to a number of figures who opened up my eyes to the possibility of a biblical base for psychology. First, my brilliant and misunderstood uncle, Avraham Chaim Saposnik, who once asked me if I knew that the word "psyche" was of Greek origin, and challenged me to find a Hebrew alternative. Second, my historian father, Lewis C. Kaplan, who as a serious Jewish intellectual, lover of languages, and published translator taught me the discipline of serious scholarship, and my mother, Edith Saposnik Kaplan, a writer in her own right, who always urged me to be an intellectual, but a "Hebrew intellectual." Third my biblically literate uncle Joseph "Ishiah" Saposnik who provided a calm and steady influence helping make this project possible. Fourth, my son Daniel Lewis Kaplan, now a psychologist himself, who chased ping-pong balls under tables with me as we tried to model differential relationship patterns, and my daughter-in-law, Reva Nelson, who comes from a multi-generational family of rabbis. And of course my two young grandsons, Levi Judah and Isaiah Max, who are being given both an intellectual and emotional Jewish and general education.

Finally, outside of my family, I was greatly influenced and tutored in this regard by my first professor, Donald Campbell who introduced me to the work of Erich Wellisch, whose book *Isaac and Oedipus* opened my eyes, and by Professor Abram Sachar, the founding President of Brandeis University. When I came to him bemoaning the lack of a biblical presence in psychology, Professor Sachar said to me: "Create it!" *Living Biblically* represents another step in this direction.

Kalman J. Kaplan, PhD
Professor of Clinical Psychology
Director, Program of Religion, Spirituality & Mental Health
Department of Psychiatry
University of Illinois at Chicago College of Medicine
Adjunct Professor
Spertus Institute of Jewish Studies

List of Tables

Introduction

AMERICANS HAVE BEEN LIVING in recent times in an affluent society with an abundance of choices. Yet many people report feeling that their lives are aimless and without purpose and spiritually empty. Religious leaders in traditional societies often applied the psychological wisdom implicit in the biblical religious traditions to the particular life problems of members of their flock. The situation in contemporary America and the West seems to be dramatically different. At first glance it appears that psychologists and psychiatrists seem to do the majority of mental health treatment, while clergy are often reduced to purely religious, ceremonial or social duties.

In the field of psychology in particular, mental health practitioners tend to disparage belief in a creator as a delusion (an "illusion"[1] or even a "mass-delusion" as Freud famously called it[2]) or immature, and tend to avoid in therapy any reference to a patient's religious beliefs and their influence. The therapist is often ignorant of, if not antagonistic to religion, often in a manner incongruent with the patient's own orientation. More than that, the psychotherapist often fails to appreciate or even understand a serious religious approach to life.

Koenig, for example, cites surveys done in the 1980s and 1990s indicating 57–74 percent of psychologists and 24–75 percent of psychiatrists didn't believe in God, in contrast to only 4 percent of the general American public.[3] This is a huge disconnect! Most mental health professionals have traditionally avoided any reference to, or recognition of their patients' religious beliefs and the deep influence of these beliefs on patients' lives.

1. Freud, *Future of an Illusion*, 3–56.

2. Freud, *Civilization and Discontents*, 59–145.

3. Koenig, *Faith and Health*, 27; Regan et al., "Psychologists and Religion," 208–37; Shafranske and Malony, "Orientations and Practice," 72–78.

A review article by Weaver, however, suggests that clergy might play a far greater role in mental health counseling than one might think. In a review of ten separate studies, Weaver found that clergy do perform a great deal of counseling, indeed spending 10 to 20 percent of their forty- to sixty-hour work week counseling people with emotional or marital problems.[4] Koenig ingeniously applied this percentage to a 1998 Department of Labor estimate of 353,000 clergy serving congregations in the United States (including four thousand Jewish rabbis, forty-nine thousand Catholic priests and three hundred thousand Protestant pastors) and arrived at the following aggregate statistic: clergy spend approximately 138 million hours delivering mental health care each year.[5] For the approximately eighty-three thousand members of the American Psychological Association to reach such a figure would require each member to offer mental health services at a rate of 33.2 hours per week. This figure is undoubtedly higher as many of these APA members are not even clinicians! Koenig goes on to report a study of help-seeking for personal problems from 1957 to 1976. What is significant is that more Americans sought help from a clergyman than from a psychiatrist or psychologist.[6]

Yet, this does not solve the problem of the disconnect between clergy and mental health professionals either. First of all, many clergy and even practicing pastoral counselors do not have a solid base of knowledge regarding mental illness, nor of the psychological issues that their sermons may provoke. Lafuze et al., for example, report that 86 percent of 1031 mainline Methodist ministers sampled agreed that medication helps people control symptoms and manage their relationships better.[7] However, 47 percent of these same pastors incorrectly believed that psychiatric patients are "more dangerous than an average citizen," with only 24 percent in disagreement. Views of more fundamentalist or conservative clergy have yet to be determined.

Secondly, many pastoral counselors put aside their religious instincts when conducting psychotherapy, often seeming to wear two hats. Neither hat quite fits. In their zeal to treat religion as a private as opposed to a public matter, pastoral psychotherapists have often adopted a therapeutic

---

4. Weaver, "Has there been a failure," 129–47.
5. Koenig, *Faith and Health*, 173–74.
6. Veroff et al., *Mental Health*.
7. Lafuze et al., "Perceptions," 900–1.

mode that is far from neutral, but based rather on assumptions and values emerging from an implicit classical Greek view of life, leaving students interested in a serious interface of religion and mental health adrift.

A number of recent thinkers have pointed to the implicit Greek view underlying psychology and psychiatry, often to their detriment. The Norwegian clergyman Thorlief Boman[8] has attempted to differentiate Hebrew and Greek ways of thinking. While Greek thinking emphasizes seeing, the static, the logical, and the nomothetic, Hebrew thought stresses hearing, the dynamic, the psychological, and the ideographic. Phillip Slater brilliantly illustrates the pathological patterns in Greek family life. Overcoming the rampant idealization of Greek society, Slater describes the classical Greeks as "quarrelsome as friends, treacherous as neighbors, brutal as masters, faithless as servants, shallow as lovers—all of which was in part redeemed by their intelligence and creativity."[9] In a highly original work, Milton Faber[10] points to the prevalence of suicide by Greek characters in the tragedies of Sophocles and Euripides. More recently, Bennett Simon[11] has pointed out the dependence of psychiatry on Greek thinking. Yosef Yersushalmi[12] continues in the same vein, arguing that Freud himself carried the Greek cyclical view of history and sense of hopelessness into psychoanalysis.

An interesting pattern emerges. Although Freud clearly dismissed religion as a "mass delusion," his hostility seemed largely focused on biblical legends (which he seems to define as religious) and not on Greek myths such as Oedipus and Narcissus, which he seems so enamored of (and which themselves emerge from the Pantheon of Greek gods). A letter from Freud reproduced in a recent Hebrew-language work by Rolnik[13] confirms this impression. A short time after Freud's publication of *The Interpretation of Dreams*,[14] the Jewish historian and folklorist Alter Druyanov (then of Odessa) wrote to Freud to alert him of the considerable similarity between his ideas and those of the early Hebrews. Here is Freud's answer: "I'm happy

8. Boman, *Hebrew Thought*.

9. Slater, *Glory*, 4.

10. Faber , *Suicide and Tragedy*.

11. Simon, *Mind and Madness*.

12. Yersushalmi, *Freud's Moses*.

13. Rolnik, *Freud in Zion*, 47. Thanks are due to Daniel Algom for providing the translation of the Hebrew passage.

14. Freud, *Interpretation of Dreams*.

to learn of a competent reader of my book from so far a place. As far as I'm concerned however the similarity between my ideas and those of the early Greeks strikes me as much more salient."

The effects of Freud's anti-biblical bias are still apparent in psychology and psychiatry. The Scriptures are filled with rich, psychological stories involving relations between parents and children, husbands and wives, and the individual and God. A problem is that the Bible is a difficult book to read and apply in one's own life. Oftentimes theology and elaborative interpretive commentary come between the biblical narrative and the reader. Whatever the reason, modern psychology and psychiatry have made very little use of biblical materials, being implicitly based on a classical Greek view of mental life. Most psychologists, psychoanalysts, social workers, and even pastoral counselors learn a psychology based on the Freudian system—psychosexual stages, Oedipus Complex, narcissism, and the like. This is true even for newer approaches, such as client-centered, existential, humanistic, and even multicultural approaches, which seem to implicitly reflect this often unwitting enmeshment and fixation in classical Greek myth, religion, and thought. Modern human beings, and perhaps especially mental health professionals, are akin to fish swimming in a orange-tinted tank and concluding that the waters of the world are orange.

A shining exception in this regard is Dr. Eric Wellisch, medical director of Grayford Child Guidance Clinic in England, who over fifty years ago called for a biblical psychology, arguing that

> The very word "psyche" is Greek. The central psychoanalytic concept of the formation of character and neurosis is shaped after the Greek Oedipus myth. It is undoubtedly true that the Greek thinkers possessed an understanding of the human mind which, in some respects, is unsurpassed to the present day, and that the trilogy of Sophocles still presents us with the most challenging problems. But stirring as these problems are, they were not solved in the tragedy of Oedipus. In ancient Greek philosophy, only a heroic fight for the solution but no real solution is possible. Ancient Greek philosophy has not the vision of salvation.
>
> No positive use has been made, so far, of the leading ideas of Biblical belief in the attempts of modern psychology to formulate basic findings and theories. But there is no reason why the Bible should not prove at least if not more fruitful than the concepts of Greek or Eastern religious experience . . . Psychology and theology are at the crossroads. The atheistic and pantheistic aspects of

modern psychology lead to dangerous conclusions . . . The non-biological aspect of theology is doomed to lead to frustration. There is need for a Biblical psychology.[15]

The emerging field of biblical psychology is somewhat unique in being driven by clientele and patients rather than simply by professionals. In addition, it has the potential of transcending the limitations of earlier waves of psychology. It differs from both psychodynamic theory and behaviorism in its emphasis on the integration of inner processes and outer behavior. It differs from humanistic psychology, in being open to biblical Hebrew rather than European Greek humanism,[16] and thus to the spiritual concerns of faith communities. Finally it transcends multi-cultural psychology by trying to identify the universal processes intrinsic to human life itself as they are manifested in particular culturally-specific areas of behavior.

In a series of books on religion and mental health, I along with Matthew Schwartz and Moriah Markus-Kaplan,[17] have begun to develop a biblical psychology. The present book applies this thinking systematically to ten issues of daily life: 1) Relating to the Environment, 2) Relating to Another as Yourself, 3) Relating to Authority, 4) Relating to a the Opposite Sex, 5) Relating to a Son, 6) Relating to a Daughter, 7) Relating to Siblings, 8) Relating Body to Soul, 9) Relating to a Self-Destructive Person, and 10) Relating to Misfortune.

In each case, the Greek narratives leave people trapped, or worse, resulting in unsatisfactory attempts to reach positive psychological accommodations. The Greek narratives regarding each of the above issues make abundantly clear that it is impossible to escape one's fate, no matter how hard one tries, in order to achieve constructive accommodations. Sadly, Greek characters find their attempts at resolution to be fruitless, destructive, and sometimes even fatal.

Unfortunately, modern psychology and psychiatry have been dependent, implicitly or explicitly, on this ancient Greek worldview. In this tragic Greek view, protagonists are done in by immutable and unchangeable character flaws. In Shakespeare's tragedies, for example, Macbeth

15. Wellisch, *Isaac and Oedipus*, 115.

16. Buber, *Israel and World*.

17. Kaplan, *TILT*; Kaplan et al., *Family*; Kaplan and Schwartz, *Seven Habits*; Kaplan and Schwartz, *Psychology of Hope*; Schwartz and Kaplan, *Biblical Stories*; Schwartz and Kaplan, *Fruit of Her Hands*.

is done in by ambition, Othello by jealousy, Hamlet by indecision, and Coriolanus by a kind of rigidity. All their attempts at change are for naught, and they wind up spinning their wheels, cycling back and forth, often brilliantly, yet fruitlessly. Yet intellectual society seems to revel in this tragic view of life, ignoring the simpler yet more profound solutions emerging from biblical narratives.

In this book we will suggest contrasting biblical narratives for each of the ten life issues listed above, allowing for constructive resolutions. What is common to all of them is the sense that people are not stuck, change is possible, and life is of intrinsic value. In the biblical world, people are not trapped. They can and do grow, develop, and sometimes even change. We offer biblical resolutions to these life issues that can help the readers live happier and more fulfilled lives. They represent guides for therapists, counselors, coaches, and laypeople themselves, in how to avoid the psychological traps set up in Greek narratives, and to live biblically.

Now let us begin.

1

Relating to the Environment

PSYCHO-BIBLICAL ISSUE ONE:

What should my relationship to the environment be? Can I change any part of the environment or must I leave it exactly the way it is?

THE GREEK AND BIBLICAL creation stories embody two radically different worldviews. Nature precedes the gods in the Greek version, but God precedes nature in the account. The differences in the respective orderings are not just chronological, but logical and psychological as well.[1]

The Greek Narrative

According to Hesiod, in the beginning there was Chaos, which has often been interpreted as a moving formless mass, from which the cosmos and the gods originated.[2] The noun "*xaos*" refers to infinite space or time or the nether abyss while the verb "*xao*" denotes "to destroy utterly."[3] Chaos has come to mean complete disorder and confusion, a far cry from the formlessness implied by *tohu vovohu* in the biblical story of creation.

---

1. Snell, *Discovery of the Mind.*
2. Hesiod, *Theogony*, line 116.
3. Liddell and Scott, *Lexicon.*

There is the implication chaos must be subdued and controlled for the world to be formed.

In the Olympian theogony, nature exists before the gods. The male Sky (Ouranos) impregnates the female Earth (Gaia) and produces first the hundred-handed monsters and then the Cyclopes. The family pathology then immediately commences, as the father takes the children away from the mother. "Sky tied them (the Cyclopes) up and threw them into Tartarus, a dark and gloomy place in Hades as far from earth as earth is from the sky, and again had children by Earth, the so-called Titans." Such action of course breeds reaction, and Earth repays Sky in spades.

> Grieved at the loss of the children who were thrown into Tartarus, Earth persuaded the Titans to attack their father and gave Cronus a steel sickle . . . Cronus cut off his father's genitals and threw them into the sea . . . Having thus eliminated their Father the Titans brought back their brother who had been hurled to Tartarus and gave the rule to Cronus.[4]

Thus, the Oedipal conflict is born, and indeed, ingrained through the Furies into the fabric of the natural world. Indeed, it seems to be an unchanging law of nature, foretold by Earth and Sky. When Earth and Sky foretold that Cronus would lose the rule to his own son, he devoured his offspring as they were born. The infant Zeus is saved through a ruse. When Zeus reaches adulthood he makes war on Cronus and the Titans, and defeats Cronus, fulfilling the prophecy of Earth and Sky. The drama of infanticide continues. Zeus himself is informed that his own son would displace him. To forestall this, he devoured his wife with the embryo in her womb. Nevertheless, Zeus is not all powerful, subject himself to the natural force of Necessity, which itself is controlled by the Fates and the Furies.[5]

Prometheus ("forethought" in Greek) and Epimetheus ("afterthought"), cousins of Zeus, who joined him in his war against his father Cronus, are assigned the responsibility of creating man. Prometheus shapes man out of mud and Athena, daughter of Zeus, breathes life into them. Prometheus assigned Epimetheus the task of giving the creatures of the Earth their various qualities, such as swiftness, cunning, strength, fur, wings. Unfortunately, by the time he got to man, Epimetheus had given out all the good qualities and there were none left for man. So Prometheus

---

4. Apollodorus, *Library,* 1.1.4.
5. Ibid., 1.1.5, 1.2.1, 1.3.6; Aeschylus, *Prometheus Bound,* lines 514–17.

decided to "make man stand erect, bidding him look up to the heaven, and lift his head to the stars."[6]

Yet Zeus has become enraged that Prometheus outwitted him into taking the white bones of a great ox concealed in folds of white fat, while first hiding and then giving to men the meaty parts, thick with fat. Zeus in retaliation decides to keep man subservient and thus withholds the knowledge of fire. But Prometheus steals fire, and hiding it in a hollow fennel stalk, gives it to man, enabling him to gain autonomy and have some constructive mastery with regard to his environment. Zeus, however, becomes furious over Prometheus's theft of fire. In order to punish man, Zeus commissions his son Hephaestus to create a trap for man— woman, Pandora, a mortal of stunning beauty endowed with many gifts, a deceptive heart, and a lying tongue, who is described as a "race apart." She opens an urn that Zeus has sent with her, which unleashes all the ills and evils unto the world, leaving hope alone locked in the now closed urn.[7] All because Prometheus has dared to steal the secret of fire that Zeus has tried to withhold from man.

It is almost impossible to overestimate the importance of fire to human beings. Primitive human beings were dominated by nature. Day and night are different worlds. The sunlight of day provides human beings with light and heat. It enables them to distinguish land from water, friendly animals and people from predatory and dangerous ones, and provides relief from the cold. At night, the sun hides, and man is rendered helpless. But fire changes all this. It generates light and heat to hold the environment at bay. Fire enables man to separate the light from the dark and civilization from wilderness. It also enables him to forge and sharpen weapons and cooking utensils, make wheels and medicinal treatments, and cook and sanitize food. It enables the human being to constructively make his environment more inhabitable.

How do these stories impact on the Greek and later Roman relationships with the earth? There is no simple answer to this question. When we examine the evidence, we see a peculiar ambivalence. On the one hand, Earth, *Gaia*, was seen as the mother of gods, humans, and every living thing.[8] As such, she was to be worshiped and not altered in any way that

6. Ovid, *Metamorphoses,* lines 76–86.

7. Hesiod, *Theogony,* lines 534–55, 558–64, 565–69, 570–605.

8. Hesiod, *Homeric Hymns,* 30.1.

would upset an abstract balance. On the other hand, many of her off-spring were monsters, and her fecundity had a dark side.

As evidence for the idealizing pole, the environmental historian J. Donald Hughes argues that "the Greeks in particular thought that rearranging land and sea was a prideful challenge to Zeus, who had ratified their limits when he divided the world with his brothers."[9] Hughes offers the following example to support this thesis. When the people of Cnidus tried to dig a canal through the neck of land that connected them to Asia Minor, many injuries occurred to the workmen from flying rock splinters. They received the following explanation from the Oracle of Delphi: "Do not fence off the isthmus, do not dig. Zeus would have made an island had he willed it."[10] They stopped work immediately.

Hughes provides another example to support his case regarding what is at times the Greek unwillingness to alter the earth at all. During the invasion of Greece by the Persian king Xerxes, it was regarded as evidence of "pride going before a fall" that he had built a bridge of boats across the Hellespont, turning sea into land, and that he caused a canal to be cut through the Athos peninsula.[11]

On the other hand, the Greek attitudes towards the earth sometimes seemed to go to the opposite extreme. Greek farmers seemed to be aware of how to treat the soil[12] and the importance of fallowing the land and of crop rotation, in which soil-restoring legumes were planted in alternate years with other crops.[13] Yet Hughes suggests that "their use in the Mediterranean was limited by the small size of farms and the necessity of planting each species only where soil and exposure would favor it."[14] In many ways, the Greeks, and later the Romans, seemed to have been quite indifferent regarding certain ravages to their environment. Hughes points in particular to the problems of deforestation, overgrazing and erosion. Plato, for example observed that the heavily forested mountains of Attica had been laid bare by the cutting of timber and by grazing, resulting

9. Hughes, *Pan's Travail*, 51.

10. Herodotus, *Histories,* 1.174.

11. Strabo, *Geographica,* 14.2.5.

12. Hesiod, *Works and Days,* line 464; Xenophon, *Economist,* 5–12; White, *Roman Farming,* 177.

13. Theophrastus, *Causis Plantarum,* 4.7.3, 4.8.1–3; *Enquiry,* 8.11.8.

14. Vergil, *Georgics,* lines 73–75; Pliny the Elder, *Natural History,* 18.91; Hughes, *Pan's Travail,* 139–40.

in an erosion of the rich and deep soil. As a consequence, the springs and streams had dried up.[15] Strabo offered a similar analysis, maintaining that the forests near Pisa had been exhausted by shipbuilding and the construction of buildings in Rome and villas in the surrounding countryside.[16]

The depletion of wildlife was also a problem and is reflected in the ambivalent Greek attitude towards the nature deity Artemis (adopted into the Roman pantheon as Diana). On the one hand, she was a protectress of wild animals, on the other, a hunter of them. According to a Greek myth, the mighty hunter Orion boasted that he would kill every wild beast in the world. In retaliation, Artemis, goddess of the wild, or in some versions, Gaia, mother earth herself, retaliated by sending a giant scorpion to sting Orion. Zeus intervened and set both Orion and the scorpion in the sky as constellations opposite one another.[17] This certainly indicates a Greek awareness that wildlife might be destroyed. And there were attempts to protect animals within wildlife preserves. Sacrifices of wild animals as opposed to domestic animals were rare in Greek, though not in later Roman times, and wild animals in sanctuaries were preserved as sacred to the gods.[18] Nevertheless, the Greek fascination with hunting did tend to diminish certain animal species.

The situation seems to have become worse in later Roman times though there were always important figures that stood up for animal rights. Plutarch in particular exhibited respect, admiration and sympathy for living creatures.[19] Nevertheless Hughes argues that there is considerable doubt that this translated into practical programs to protect wildlife.[20] And even more devastatingly, the later Roman Empire was the scene of numerous circuses or hecatombs within the city of Rome and in addition numerous *venationes* were held in other towns throughout the empire, wherein thousands of wild animals were massacred for the entertainment of the public.[21]

15. Plato, *Critias,* 111b-d.

16. Strabo, *Geograpica,* 5.2.5.

17. Ovid, *Fasti,* 5:539–41.

18. Apollodurus, 3.9.2.

19. Plutarch, *Morals,* 999A.

20. Hughes, *Pan's Travail,* 111.

21. Friedlander, *Life and Manners,* 2:66.

What do we make of the Greek narrative underlying these historical trends? A number of points stand out.

1. Earth and Sky exist prior to the gods and in fact create them. Chaos must be subdued for this process to occur.

2. The earth-mother is a very ambivalent source. She gives life but also destroys it. Such a view creates an ambivalent human attitude towards the environment.

3. Zeus is trying to keep man dependent, sending him woman as a punishment for him gaining fire, which would enable him to shape nature in a healthy way.

4. Man vacillates between idealizing and worshipping the earth and, conversely, ravaging and raping it.

The Biblical Narrative

The biblical account of creation is very different. God precedes and indeed creates nature in the biblical account, nature representing the rules which God has put into place to create some order in the physical world he has created. However, the All Powerful God is not bound by the rules he created (unless God desires to be bound by them)[22].

22. This is not a simple issue and I am indebted to my student Moshe Rosenwasser for the following observation. Rabbi Moshe ben Nachman (Nachmanides) argues that God performs miracles from time to time (such as the splitting of the Red Sea) that countermand nature. However, God keeps miracles rare. A plethora of miracles is unwarranted for two reasons: (a) because they are unnecessary and the same end can be accomplished through other means and (b) because the primary beneficiaries are not sufficiently deserving. Now, if miracles are rare, and nature is immutable, how does God control the universe? He does this through a combination of two Hebrew names (attributes) El and Shaddai. El means all-powerful, establishing the idea that God can do whatever he desires and that his abilities are limited by nothing. Shaddai is derived from the root Sh-D-D, which means thief.

Rosenwasser offers the following example. Since nature is so diverse and has so many contradictory crosscurrents, God can manipulate (not break, but manipulate) nature and bring about any result he desires. For example, we know that water boils at 212°F. What happens if for some reason God wishes water to boil at 200°F? All he needs to do is bring about a very low-pressure system, and that will cause the water to boil at a lower temperature (by Gay-Lussac's Law). Is this a clear miracle? No. Anyone who records the event will ascribe it to the low-pressure system. However, one righteous person may really need that boiling water, and he will know in his heart that God performed a miracle for him. So God acts like a thief, very stealthily controlling the universe, while appearing to

In contrast the Greek portrayal of Zeus as withholding fire from man, rabbinic sages portray the biblical God as providing the means for Adam to invent fire. God does this specifically because God has compassion for man.[23] And again woman is not seen as an alien force or something synonymous with an earth-mother or a race apart. She is made of the same substance as man. She is not a punishment but a blessing. Furthermore, in the second creation story in Genesis, man is specifically described as being formed from the dust of the ground. God proclaims, "It is not good for man to be alone. I will make a help-meet [literally a "helpmeet opposite" or *ezer kenegdo*] for him."[24] Woman is not described as a race apart but in fact as being taken from the rib of man. And the man said: "This is now bone of my bone, and flesh of my flesh. She shall be called Woman because she was taken out of man."[25] She is not an alien force to be worshipped or ravaged. Neither is the earth, from the biblical point of view.

In any case, the biblical view is clear. God exists prior to nature and in fact creates the heaven and the earth. "In the beginning God created the heaven and the earth." God then proceeds to create form out of the unformed (*tohu vovohu*)—again, not out of chaos as in the Greek account. The Hebrew "unformed" is not equivalent to the Greek "chaos." Therefore, nature does not have to be subdued but rather shaped. God is not seen a tyrant but as a potter, differentiating as necessary.

First, lightness is divided from darkness. God then divides water from the land. At this point, God begins to prepare this world for the entrance of man. First, God has the earth bring forth vegetation. He then places living creatures in the sea and fowls in the sky. Now God places living creatures on the earth, cattle, creeping things, and other beasts. The world is now ready for man in God's plan. God creates the human being, male and female, his ultimate handiwork, in God's own image, and gives them dominion over all in nature God has created.[26]

---

let nature take its course. All these activities are called "miracles within nature." Though God's face is hidden from us, and he appears not to acknowledge any of our deeds, God is still there, quietly and stealthily manipulating the laws of nature to achieve his desired outcome, which is caring for the human being and providing for his continued growth and development.

23. *Midrash Genesis Rabbah* 11:2.

24. Gen 2:18.

25. Gen 2.

26. Gen 1.

The Bible describes the world and all that is in it as created by God in love. Humankind is given dominion over all, and the first people are placed in the Garden of Eden "to till it and tend it."[27] It is incumbent on humanity not to wantonly destroy. Having dominion over nature does not entitle man to misuse nature. Nature is not presented as something alien to man. It is neither to be worshiped nor raped, but instead tended and cared for lovingly and carefully. The land of Israel was to lie fallow one year out of every seven, and although the purpose was not specifically the replenishment of the soil, replenishment would serve as one benefit.[28] "You shall not destroy" (lo tashchit)[29] is stated in the context of destroying trees but is understood in the rabbinic literature as including all sorts of wanton destruction. All that God created has its own purpose and beauty. Having dominion does not entitle man to misuse nature, but rather man must exercise an attitude of respect and even awe, a notion that carries over into Jewish law, which mandates individuals to recite blessings for all manner of natural phenomena (rainbow, lightning, shooting stars, the first blossoms of a tree, etc.).

Midrash[30] recounts that David once did not understand why God needed to create spiders. Then on one occasion while fleeing from King Saul, David hid in a cave. A spider quickly came along and spun a web over the entrance, saving David's life. David, after realizing what had happened, humbly corrected his misconception. Each of God's creations has a purpose.

The medieval Sefer Hachinuch[31] writes that the essence of this law is to teach people to love what is good and beneficial and to take care of it. "It is the way of pious people who love peace and rejoice in the good of the Creation that they would not destroy even a mustard seed and they will do all in their power to prevent needless destruction." In the same line of thinking, the Talmud says that one who destroys anything in anger is as though guilty of worshiping idols, in the sense that he obeys the destructive urges in his nature rather than connecting with God and the wonders of his creation.[32]

27. Gen 2:15.
28. Lev 25:2–7.
29. Deut 20:19–20.
30. *Midrash Alpha Beta Acheres d'Ben Sira* 9.
31. *Sefer Hachinuch*, 529.
32. *b. Shabbat* 105b.

On the direct practical level, there are dozens of biblical laws that regulate in great detail what we may and may not do to the environment.[33] The Hebrew Scriptures prohibit the crossbreeding of different species of animals,[34] as it bans the transplanting of branches of differing species of fruit trees,[35] and the intermingling of seeds in planting.[36] Likewise, the Hebrew Bible prohibits various forms of activities that would involve cruelty to animals.[37] We may not harness together animals of different strengths as it might create an unbearable load on the weaker one;[38] we may not pass by an animal which has collapsed under its load, but are duty bound to help it;[39] we may not slaughter a mother and its young on the same day,[40] as we may not take the fledglings while the mother bird hovers over them.[41] On three occasions, Scripture warns against cooking the kid in its mother's milk.[42]

It is clear then that nature is not to be ravaged. However, nature is not to be worshiped in the Greek sense either. There are times when trees must be cut down, in the service of human progress. This is the rabbinic understanding of the *lo taschit* verse in Deuteronomy,[43] which literally bans *only* the destruction of *fruit-bearing* trees during war. Other trees may be destroyed and cut down in order to build bulwarks against the city that wars against one.[44]

---

33. Berman, *Values*.

34. Lev 19:19.

35. Lev 19:19, as per Maimonides, *Book of Commandments*, negative commandment no. 216.

36. Deut 22:9.

37. Shochet, *Animal Life*, chapters 9, 10, and 13.

38. Deut 22:6–7.

39. Exod 23:5; Deut 22:4.

40. Lev 22:28.

41. Deut 22:6–7.

42. Deut 14:21; Exod 23:19; 34:26.

43. Deut 20:19–20. *Lo Tashchit*, the biblical prohibition against the wanton destruction of nature: "When you besiege a city for a long time, fighting against it to conquer it, you shall not destroy the trees thereof by wielding an axe against them; for you may eat of them, and you may not cut them down, for is the tree of the field a person that it should be besieged by you? Only trees which you know not to be fruit bearing trees, may you destroy and cut down; and you may build bulwarks against the city that wars against you, until it is subdued."

44. Sifrei to Deut 20:19–20 (Finkelstein edition of Sifrei Devaraim, 238–40).

Some Talmudic writings go even further in the furthering of human welfare even if it involves some destruction of the environment. Rabbi Saul Berman points to the *Gemara* in *Baba Kamma,* which suggests that protection even of fruit-growing trees may be overridden by economic need.[45] The destruction for protection of health is permissible.[46] The *Gemara* in *Shabbat* goes even further in indicating that a psychological need or a personal aesthetic preference is sufficient to justify what would otherwise constitute a wasteful use of natural resources.[47]

Yet at the same time, all in God's creation, and even the increments that other humans have made to God's world, are entitled to be protected from wanton destruction. It is God and not humanity that is the continuing owner of all the earth.[48] In short, human needs must always be balanced against environmental concerns. It should be remembered that this biblical God does not attempt to withhold the knowledge of fire from man, as has Zeus. The implication of this is clear. Man is encouraged to incrementally improve on the environment as long as he does not wantonly destroy it. This implies an attitude of respectful stewardship rather than absolutist environmentalism or, worse, blind worship of nature. Environmental concerns must always be calibrated against human needs, and in the final analysis human needs will prevail. In the words of Rabbi Joseph B. Soloveitchik, a great contemporary interpreter of Jewish law, there is an unavoidable dynamic tension between the capacity to exercise control over nature and the duty to act toward nature with a sense of fiduciary responsibility. [49]

The following points stand out in these biblical narratives:

1. God exists prior to the heaven and earth and in fact creates them. The world is unformed (*tohu vovohu*) and must be given form and structure rather than subdued.

Maimonides, too, understands the law this way in his listing of the 613 biblical commandments in *Safer Hamitzvot,* negative commandment No. 57, as well as in his fuller treatment of this legal issue in his magnum opus, the *Mishneh Torah,* Book 14, *Shofetim,* Laws of Kings 6:10.

45. *b. Baba Kamma* 91b-92a.

46. *b. Shabbat* 128b-129a.

47. Ibid., 105b, 140b.

48. *Pentateuch,* and Gen 1:26–28.

49. Soloveitchik, *Lonely Man,* 10–16.

2. Earth is not seen in sexually differentiated terms. There is no sense of an earth-mother. The biblical God creates man and woman to tender and care for the world he has created.

3. The human being need not and indeed must not worship the earth or nature. Neither is he free to rape or ravage it. These are the two sides of Greek paganism.

4. The biblical God is not seen as trying to keep man dependent. He gives man the gift of fire to enable him to help make nature inhabitable. Again, the biblical human being is neither pushed to idealize and worship nature or, conversely, to rape and ravage it.

A Contemporary Illustration

A group of anthropologists receive a research grant to spend a year in a small village in Brazil adjacent to a very lush rainforest. The villagers live in a fairly primitive condition, and find it very difficult to transport the crops they are able to grow to a market in a nearby city. A company has offered to build a road into the town, making it much easier for the townspeople to transport their crops. At the same time, a housing conglomerate has been trying to acquire some key forestland. They want to cut the forest down and build a new housing development. The anthropologists are split over these opportunities. Some are adamantly opposed to the building of the road as well as the housing development as they feel both actions will disrupt the environment and destroy the ecological integrity of the rainforest. Others advise the villagers to seize this unexpected opportunity, as it will move them quickly into the twenty-first century. A third group advises the villagers to accept the offer of road-building, as this would be a constructive change to the environment, allowing them to more easily market their crops. They feel that not to do so would keep the villagers as a fossil, not being able to improve themselves through the advances of new technology. However, this third group opposes the housing development project on the grounds that this would represent a ravaging of the environment.

Which group would you listen to? The villagers follow the advice of the third group. They accept the offer to build a road but reject the offer for the housing development. Do you think they are right? They feel the first group of anthropologists idealizes the primitive at the expense of the villagers, and feel the second group has no respect for the environment, willing to ravage the ecosystem for a quick profit. Do you agree with them?

PSYCHO-BIBLICAL GUIDE ONE

God creates heaven and earth. Earth and Sky do not beget the gods. Belief in God frees man from enslavement by nature. Do not worship nature nor ravage it. There is no reason not to improve it or develop it as long as you do not seek to destroy it.

2

Relating to Another as Yourself

PSYCHO-BIBLICAL ISSUE TWO:

How can I keep from losing my identity in my close relationships? I sometimes feel smothered when I get too close to another and yet get very lonely when I am not in a relationship.

GREEK AND BIBLICAL NARRATIVES offer two contrasting worldviews regarding the relationship of self and other. In the Greek view, self and other seem to be in basic opposition. One wins at the expense of the other losing, and vice-versa. Indeed much of Greek life seems to be turned into a contest. It begins in athletic contests over physical prowess but extends to the realm of intellect, to feats of poetry and dramatic competition.[1] The ancient Greeks staged contests in anything and everything—beauty (male, of course), singing, riddle-solving, drinking, staying awake.[2] Everything is seen as a zero-sum game. What is at stake is the redistribution of resources rather than any increase in their total.[3] Nothing has any meaning unless it includes the defeat of another.[4]

---

1. Finley, *World of Odysseus*, 128–29.
2. Huizinga, *Homo Ludens*, 73.
3. Gouldner, *Enter Plato*, 52–57.
4. Slater, *Glory of Hera*, 36–37.

Further the Greek view of a hopeless cycle in human affairs is always not far beneath the surface. Agamemnon declares this very clearly at the beginning of Euripides' tragedy *Iphigenia in Aulis*. Hubris is followed by nemesis, and every human is born to grief.[5]

The biblical narratives offer the promise of integration of self and other and of human progress. Not everything is seen as a contest, and not everything should be seen as a zero-sum game. The patriarch, Jacob, for example provides a unique blessing for each of his sons[6]. Jacob's blessing for one son does not necessarily decrease his blessing for any other son.

Perhaps this is what makes the biblical narrative of Cain and Abel so striking. Although God accepts Abel's offering and does not accept Cain's, he makes it clear to Cain that his offering is being judged on its own terms and not in relation to Abel's. "Why are thou wroth and why is thy countenance fallen. If thou doest well, shall it not be lifted up?"[7] There is no indication in the text that God could not have accepted the sacrifices of both Cain and Abel. Yet Cain seems to interpret this as a competition against Abel and he slays him.

When God asks Cain: "Where is Abel thy brother?" Cain responds, "I know not; am I my brother's keeper?" Cain could have answered simply, "I know not," but his addition "Am I my brother's keeper?" reveals his obsession with Abel. Cain interprets God's rejection of his offering in a classical Greek rather than a biblical way. He feels he is in a contest with Abel. He has lost to Abel, and out of jealousy and anger, he slays him.

The commandment "to love your neighbor as yourself" is repeated throughout the Hebrew Bible and the Christian New Testament.[8] Although this is commonly interpreted as directing us to love another the way we love ourselves,[9] we suggest here a slightly alternate reading: to love another *as* ourselves, i.e., as individuated and developed personalities

---

5. Euripides, *Iphigenia*, lines 162–63, 442–45.

6. Gen 48–49. In actuality, Jacob blesses his two grandsons Ephraim and Manasseh as well.

7. Gen 4:1–15.

8. Lev 19:18, 34; Matt 19:19; 22:39; Mark 12:31, 33; Luke 10:27; Rom 13:9; Gal 5:14; Eph 5:33; Jas 2:9.

9. Rabbi Hillel's version of the Golden Rule is instructive here: "One should not treat others in ways that one would not like to be treated." Or "What is hateful to you, do not do to your neighbor. This is the whole Torah; all the rest is commentary. Go and learn it." *b. Shabbat* 31a

rather than as stick-figures. And of course, the biblical narratives always offer hope and purpose. "For everything there is a season, a time for every purpose under heaven."[10]

The Greek Narrative

Greek thought sees self and other as fundamentally opposed. The legend of Narcissus is prototypical in this regard. Narcissus is born out of the rape of his mother by a river-god. His mother is told by a seer that Narcissus will live a long life as long as he does not know himself.[11] Narcissus's life thus begins with an insoluble riddle. He is filled with a primordial guilt and ignorance regarding his own origins, and he must avoid self-knowledge, or die.

The Greeks often seem to see self-knowledge and awareness as unleashing a destructive secret that would better remain hidden. We see this attitude expressed throughout Sophocles' great tragedy, *Oedipus Rex*. The play begins with a priest of Zeus telling the now King Oedipus of the ravages of the plague on the city of Thebes. Creon, the brother of Jocasta (Oedipus's mother-wife) announces that the plague is due to the unavenged murder of the late King Laius and describes the circumstances surrounding that unresolved crime. Oedipus volunteers to reopen the search for the murderer of Laius, cursing the killer to a life of misery and solitude. Oedipus summons Tiresias, the blind oracle, who points to the dangers of self-knowledge. "Alas, how dreadful to have wisdom where it profits not the wise!"[12]

In her last line, much later in the play, Jocasta similarly warns Oedipus of the danger in the search for his identity; "Ill-fated one! Mayest thou never come to know who thou art!" She then walks off-stage for the last time and hangs herself. A plethora of destructive acts follow in both *Oedipus Rex* and other plays of Sophocles and Aeschylus. Oedipus blinds himself, his two sons kill each other at the Seventh Gate of Thebes, his daughter Antigone is buried alive and subsequently hangs herself, her suitor Haemon stabs himself after unsuccessfully trying to kill his father, and finally Haemon's mother stabs herself after finding him dead[13].

10. Eccl 3:1.

11. Ovid, *Metamorphoses*, 3.

12. Sophocles, *Oedipus Rex*, lines 316–17.

13. Ibid., 1068–69, 1373–77; Aeschylus, *Seven Against Thebes,* lines 879–924;

The story of Narcissus follows a cyclical Greek view of time. Although many fall in love with Narcissus, he heartlessly rejects lovers of both sexes. His lack of inner knowledge is masked by a stubborn pride (hubris) in his own beauty. Among these lovers is Echo, who has no voice of her own and can only reflect back what Narcissus says.[14]

One of those whom Narcissus has scorned raises his hands to heaven and prays: "May he, himself, fall in love with another, as we have done with him; may he, too, be unable to gain his loved one!" Nemesis, hearing this prayer, causes Narcissus to seek shelter from the sun near a pool and to fall in love with his own reflection in it. At first, Narcissus unsuccessfully tries to embrace and kiss the beautiful boy who confronts him.[15]

Suddenly, however, he recognizes the face in the brook as his own. It his double or *doppelganger*.[16] Narcissus lies gazing at his image for hours. Desiring to separate his soul from his body, he seeks a "joint death." "Alas! I am myself the boy I see . . . I am on fire with love for my own self. My very plenty makes me poor. How I wish I could separate myself from my body! I have no quarrel with death, for in death I shall forget my pain: but I could wish that the object of my love might outlive me: as it is, both of us will perish together when this one life is destroyed."[17]

Grief is destroying him, yet he rejoices in the knowledge that his other self will remain true to him. Saying "alas" (which Echo repeats), Narcissus pines away unto death, mourning the boy he loves in vain. "His last words as he gazed into the familiar waters were 'Woe is me for the boy I loved in vain!' . . . When he said his last farewell, "Farewell!" said Echo too. He laid down his weary head on the green grass, and death closed the eyes which so admired their owner's beauty."[18] Conon's account of the myth ends with a more active suicide; Narcissus plunges a dagger into his breast.[19]

To briefly recapitulate, Narcissus is totally self-involved, heartlessly rejecting would-be lovers of both sexes. A rejected suitor prays that Narcissus himself will experience unrequited love. Nemesis answers this

Sophocles, *Antigone*, lines 925, 1221–23, 1225–35, 1287–1302.

14. Ovid, *Metamorphoses,* 3.359–92.

15. Ibid., 3. 405–6, 3.414–54.

16. Rank, *Double.*

17. Ovid, *Metamorphoses,* 3.463–75.

18. Ibid., 3.497–502.

19. Conon, *Narrationes,* 24.

prayer, causing Narcissus, for the first time, to fall hopelessly in love. He now idealizes the face in the brook, not realizing that it represents his own reflection. Ultimately, however, Narcissus recognizes the face in the brook is his own. He is not self-invested, but self-empty, driven to grasp his missing self, which has now been projected onto the outside world. "Alas! I am myself the boy I see . . . I am on fire for love of my own self." Such a psychotic juxtaposition rips Narcissus apart and he commits suicide.

What do we make of this Greek narrative? A number of points stand out.

1. Narcissus is born of a dysfunctional relationship and must avoid self-knowledge or die. This is typical of Greek thinking.

2. He initially rejects others in interests of self-grandiosity, concealing the psychic fact that he lacks a self-identity.

3. He ultimately loses his self in an infatuation with a face in a brook (his double).

4. Narcissus comes to recognize the face in the brook as his missing self. Rather than help him integrate self and other, this knowledge makes this opposition even more profound and leads to his splitting apart psychologically and dying.

The Biblical Narrative

Consider, by contrast, the biblical book of Jonah. Jonah is confused and conflicted several times during the narrative. In fact, he expresses the wish to die on several occasions, but he does not commit suicide. Here is an outline of his story: Jonah is ordered by God to go warn Nineveh of its wickedness. Jonah attempts to avoid God by running away to Tarshish. God sends a great wind after him, endangering his ship. When asked his identity by his shipmaster, Jonah admits to being the cause of the storm. He then asks his shipmates to throw him into the sea so as to spare themselves: "And he said to them, 'Pick me up and throw me into the sea; then the sea will become calm for you. For I know that this great tempest is because of me.'" They do so, and while the ship is thus saved, Jonah is also saved—a great fish sent by God swallows him and saves him from drowning.[20]

20. Jonah 1.

While Jonah is in the belly of the fish, he prays to God. After three days, the fish vomits Jonah out safely on to dry land:

> Then Jonah prayed to the Lord his God from the fish's belly . . . "For You cast me into the depth, into the heart of the seas, and the floods surrounded me; all Your billows and Your waves passed over me. Then I said: 'I have been cast out of Your sight'; yet I will look again toward Your holy temple . . . I will pay what I have vowed. Salvation is of the Lord." So the Lord spoke to the fish, and it vomited Jonah onto dry land.[21]

Once again, God commands Jonah to go to Nineveh. This time Jonah does go and gives the people of Nineveh God's message. They repent and are saved. Jonah is angry, however, and desires to die: "But it displeased Jonah exceedingly, and he became angry . . . 'Therefore now, O Lord, please take my life from me; for it is better for me to die than to live!'"[22]

Jonah leaves the city to sit on its outskirts. There he is shielded by a gourd plant that God makes to grow up over him. "And the Lord God prepared a plant and made it come up over Jonah, that it might be a shade for his head to deliver him from his misery. So Jonah was very grateful for the plant."[23]

God then destroys the plant with a worm, exposing Jonah to the sun. Jonah again expresses the wish to die: "And the sun beat on Jonah's head, so that he grew faint. Then he wished death for himself, and said, 'It is better for me to die than to live.'"[24]

God again intervenes, asking Jonah, "Is it right for you to be angry about the plant?" When Jonah replies, "It is right for me to be angry, even to death." God uses the opportunity to explain the meaning of divine mercy:

> You have had pity on the plant for which you have not labored, nor made it grow, which came up in a night and perished in a night. And should I not pity Nineveh, that great city, in which are more than one hundred twenty thousand persons who cannot discern between their right hand and their left hand—and also much livestock?[25]

The method God uses to impart this teaching is a deeply important part of the lesson. Rather than rebuke Jonah directly and impatiently as

21. Jonah 2.
22. Jonah 3:1–10; 4:1–3.
23. Jonah 4:6.
24. Jonah 4:7–8.
25. Jonah 4:9–11.

would seem fitting at this point, God behaves as a skilled therapist in offering a parable about a plant. This kind of intervention avoids wounding Jonah and making him defensive. This enables Jonah to grow in empathy, a clear step in his development.

In summary, the story of Jonah begins with him placed in a terrible dilemma. God calls on Jonah to go to warn the people of Nineveh of their wickedness. However, Jonah does not want to go but he is too God-fearing to defy the command and too strong-willed to submit. He runs away in confusion to Tarshish and tells his shipmates to throw him overboard. The story could thus end in Jonah's suicide, *but it doesn't*—God intervenes as a protective parent, swallowing Jonah in the protective stomach of a great fish until he overcomes his confusion. Jonah prays to God from the belly of the fish until he becomes stronger. Then the fish vomits him out on dry land.

This same pattern repeats itself. God again asks Jonah to go to Nineveh. This time Jonah goes and gives the people God's message. They repent and are saved. Jonah becomes angry and again expresses the wish to die and leaves the city to sit on its outskirts. Again, God intervenes, sheltering Jonah with a gourd from the burning sun. After a worm destroys the protective gourd, Jonah once again expresses a suicidal thought. God once again intervenes, this time engaging Jonah in a mature dialogue to teach him the message of *teshuvah*, repentance or return and divine mercy and that he can reach out to another without losing himself. In the words of Hillel, "If I am not for myself, who will be for me? If I am for myself only, what am I?"[26]

The following points stand out in this biblical narrative:

1. Jonah is called by God to warn the evil people of Nineveh to change their ways. Jonah does not want to do this, nor does he want to disobey God and refuse to go. Instead, he runs away in confusion to Tarshish (to avoid being forced to choose between self and other).

2. God saves him when he jumps into the sea by placing him in the belly of a big fish. As he strengthens his identity, he is spit onto dry land.

3. Jonah does travel to warn the people of Nineveh, and again becomes suicidal, perhaps because he feels he is losing himself.

4. God protects him again from the sun with a gourd, and ultimately teaches Jonah the lesson of how he can be himself and still warn the people of Nineveh.

26. *b. Avot* 1:14.

A Contemporary Illustration

According to the ancient Greek view, intimacy with another is only achieved at the price of loss of self and space for oneself is only achieved at the expense of isolation. This very restricted view opens the door to all sorts of possible confusions and misinterpretations. Does one seek the company of others because of a genuine concern for them (let us call this *attachment*), or because of a desire to run away from oneself (let us call this *deindividuation*). Consider the following clinical example:

Rich, age 28, came to marriage therapy focusing on a lack of direction in his life. His complaint that he did not know "where he was going or who he really was" did not seem in character with his behavior with his wife. On the surface Rich seemed affectionate and eager to spend time with his wife. As therapy progressed, however, it became clear that Rich manifested an "infantile clingingness." Seemingly trivial separations became the occasion for panic responses by Rich. The initial impression that Rich was affectionate—i.e., attached—was replaced by a sense that Rich did not know who he was—a lack of *individuation*.

Likewise "farness" is open to several interpretations. Does one seek solitude to come to know oneself (*individuation*) or because of a fear of being involved with the other (*detachment*)? Consider a second clinical example:

Barbara, age 23, entered individual treatment complaining that she did not have close friends. This seemed initially to be a strange complaint because she always seemed to be surrounded by people—both male and female—and immersed in activities. However, in the course of therapy it became clear that she organized her schedule so as to minimize the possibilities for intimate contacts. In fact, she often went to desperate lengths to avoid one-on-one encounters. A superficial analysis suggested that Barbara was individuated. Closer examination, however, reveals an underlying fear of attachment.

The idea that caring for self and caring for other are contradictory has led to very ineffective attempts to correct maladies. One such solution involves the prescribing the person the opposite of what he/she has been doing. For a person overly involved with self, a prescription may involve concentrating only on the other, and vice versa. Or a compromise solution may involve trying to achieve an arithmetic balance between self and other that does not penetrate to the root of the problem.

Consider Ben, a young attorney who has been dating Laura. It is October and Laura's birthday, but Ben is very busy with a trial. Ben sends his secretary out to get some flowers for Laura, the whole process taking no longer than thirty minutes. When Ben presents the flowers to Laura, she thanks him, but her disappointment is tangible. She expected something less perfunctory. Ben feels guilty, feels he let Laura down, and resolves to behave differently the next occasion the need for a gift arises.

Soon it is February and Valentine's Day. This time Ben resolves to do it right. Though he is very busy preparing for another trial, he sets aside an entire week to look for a present for Laura. He knows she likes carpets and he looks in one store after another to search for a carpet that Laura will like. When he finally chooses one, he presents it to Laura, and she is quite happy. However, Ben does not feel so happy. He feels resentful—he has wasted forty hours of work looking for something that he is really not personally involved with. And Ben takes it out on Laura—in all ways. He comes late for his appointment, criticizes her hairstyle, and generally behaves in a very hateful way.

When Laura's next birthday arrives, Ben is in a quandary. He concludes that looking thirty minutes for a present was too little involvement (leaving him feeling guilty) and forty hours was too much (leaving him feeling like a martyr). So he decides to split the difference. He will look for twenty hours for a present for Laura—not too many (forty hours) and not too little (thirty minutes), but a halfway solution. He looks for a quilt that he thinks Laura will like, but decides to put a limit on how much time he will allot for this. He gets something, which is kind-of nice, and Laura kind-of likes it. Laura is lukewarm about the gift and Ben in turn feels lukewarm about his efforts. He does not feel too guilty and on the other hand does not feel too martyred. Neither Laura nor Ben feels taken advantage of, however neither of them feels especially satisfied either.

This is obviously not an ideal solution to the dilemma of self and other. Yet this halfway solution is exactly what many contemporary therapists have recommended. The family therapist Salvador Minuchin[27] describes the points of interchange between one member of a family and another. One type of family is enmeshed or overinvolved: it has diffuse boundaries. Such a family has difficulty providing sufficient privacy. A disengaged or underinvolved family, in contrast, is described as having rigid boundaries. This type of family should have difficulty promoting

27. Minuchin, *Families and Therapy*.

sufficient communication or intimacy. Minuchin sees healthy families as having clear boundaries, lying in the middle between diffuse boundaries and rigid boundaries. This family should allow for both some privacy and also some communication and intimacy. One should love, but one should not love too much. Not loving enough means the loss of another, but loving too much means a loss of one's self. Thus, Ben's solution of looking for twenty hours represents this sort of compromise.

However, this compromise is not really satisfactory. What is wrong with this picture? Simply, love of self is not contradictory to love of other. This of course is the psycho-biblical message. Ben is not really doing what he wants with his time and Laura is not really getting what she wants. The question becomes: What does Ben want to do with his time? What does Laura want as a gift?

One is never stronger than when one loves and is loved. Let us repeat the axiom from Rabbi Hillel cited above: "If I am not for myself, who will be for me? If I am for myself only, what am I? If not now, when?" What do these words mean? This idea has been the centerpiece of the author's bidimensional model of individuation (the ability to stand on one's own feet) and attachment (the ability to reach out one's hand to another). In this view individuation is not equivalent to detachment nor is attachment equivalent to deindividuation.[28]

From Ben's point of view, he values time that is self-expressive and avoids time that is not. What does this mean? What is self-expressive time? It is time in which one expresses something about oneself, whether it involves performing in athletics, writing, singing, building a table, cooking, making love, or composing a poem. For Ben, it may involve something to do with his song-writing ability. If he can use his time developing something of this, he will not feel it as a waste, but as expressive well-spent time. If he can give a gift to Laura that expresses him, he will not feel the opposition between self and other. The time Ben spends writing Laura a song will be experienced by him as self-expressive. The more time he spends (within limits, of course), the better he will feel about himself. He does not have to "nickel and dime" Laura with regard to how much he gives. Why? Because Ben's giving to Laura involves strengthening his own personality. Ben is never more himself than when he expresses his love for Laura.

28. Kaplan, *TILT*.

Now, what of Laura? She will value a gift that expresses care on the part of Ben. If Ben gives Laura a song that he has written specifically and expressly for her, she is likely to be very touched. Laura will likely feel that Ben cares enough to really give of himself to her. The opposition of self and other and the implicit struggle over time is broken! Ben's sense of self is not depleted by his love for Laura. Indeed it is strengthened by his expression of love toward her. And receiving his gift strengthens her sense of self.

So it is with our relationship with God. The Bible begins with a supreme act of love—God's creation of the world. In the biblical account, God created the world and human kind in an act of supreme love and kindness and has continued to deal with the world in this way ever since. One has only to look at the beauty of creation to feel God's kindness all around—as he maintains the movements of heavenly bodies and supplies the wants of even the least of his creatures. When a person truly recognizes the greatness of God's creation and the depth of his love and kindness, he cannot help but be moved to love the Creator who gave him all these wonders as an act of pure love. Indeed, the Bible expresses this human need in the form of a commandment: "And you shall love the lord your God with all your heart and with all your soul and with all your might."

Yet much in modern thought (whether eastern or western) counsels either implicitly or explicitly against loving too much for fear of excessive attachment. Loving too much is seen as engendering possessiveness, where it is feared that the lover cannot give the loved object any freedom or respect his/her individuality. Loving too much is seen as depleting ourselves, as if we are pieces of sugar that will melt through loving God or another human being.

Perhaps as a result of this, we have come to fear deep love and have come to use the term "love" so loosely as to lose its original meaning. People feel more comfortable saying that they love ice cream or their new shoes than expressing their feelings toward significant people in their lives or toward a Creator. We have implicitly accepted the idea of a compromise solution: love neither too little nor too much. Love of God or another human being is seen as in opposition to one's self. If we love God too much, we lose ourselves. If we love ourselves too much, we lose God. We search for a compromise, never realizing the solution lies right before our noses. Loving God allows us to love ourselves in a healthy manner! And then we can love God and others even more as we become more and more ourselves.[29]

PSYCHO-BIBLICAL GUIDE TWO

Love thy neighbor as thyself (Be self-expressive). Self and other are not necessarily in opposition (Narcissus), but can ultimately work in harmony (Jonah). Healthy life follows a developmental (Jonah) rather than a cyclical (Narcissus) path. It is important to learn to love another in a self-expressive way.

29. Kaplan et. al. ("Individuation and attachment") report empirical differences in individuation-attachment patterns among religious and nonreligious Jews and Buddhists. Religious Jews show high degrees of the pattern of individuated attachment advocated by Rabbi Hillel discussed previously. Religious Buddhists in comparison tend to display patterns of detached compassion, a pattern arising out of the Buddhist conception that worldly attachments leads to suffering (Muzika, *Theory, Buddhism and Self*, 59–74).

3

Relating to an Authority

PSYCHO-BIBLICAL ISSUE THREE:

How do I know whether to obey or disobey an authority figure? I sometimes feel authority figures are not to be trusted and do not have my best interests at heart.

WHETHER ONE SHOULD OBEY an authority or disobey it and even rebel against it is one of the most vexing questions in society. A widely cited series of experiments by the late social psychologist Stanley Milgram has attempted to demonstrate the dangers of obedience. In his basic study, (presented as an experiment in "paired associate learning"), over half of the "teachers" (in reality the subjects of the experiment), think they are applying mild to moderate to severe and even dangerous and life-threatening electric shocks to the "learner" (actually the experimental confederate), who has actually stated that he has a heart condition, and stops answering at a certain point.[1]

The Milgram studies were designed to model the behavior of Nazi war criminals and to belittle the defense used at Nuremberg: "We were just following orders." However, this message may have been overlearned and thus mislearned. The mantra of the West has come to be a distrust

---

1. Milgram, *Obedience.*

of *authority per se* (e.g., parents, community and religious leaders, the political structure, the legal and judicial system, and indeed any system of morality) rather than of a *particular authority*.

Yet is following orders always detrimental? The Nazi defendants at Nuremberg themselves could be viewed as actually disobeying a higher command regarding the sanctity of life that would trump an order deliberately ignoring this rule. The Israelites leaving Egypt are criticized for "not following orders" and building a golden calf.[2]

The philosopher Albert Camus[3] writes that revolt, revolution, and striving for freedom are inevitable aspects of human existence, but warns us that we must observe limits to avoid having these admirable pursuits end in tyranny. Later work in social psychology[4] analyzes both the duty to obey and the duty to disobey. The duty to obey is inherent in the very concept of authority. However, the very fact that acts of obedience can come to be regarded as crimes implies an alternative set of norms exist to disobey an unjust authority.

The moral and epistemological question becomes whether an authority is just or unjust or, more concretely, whether it is trustworthy or not and thus whether its commands should be obeyed or disobeyed. Specifically, how is this problem viewed in Greek versus biblical narratives with regard to the portrayal of Zeus/oracles versus the God of the Bible? We will contrast two narratives in this regard: 1) "creation stories" and 2) stories of "the flood." The question of obedience versus disobedience/rebellion depends on who one's authority or God is.

Greek Narratives

1. The Greek Creation Narrative

Nature precedes and creates the gods in the Olympian creation narrative. Sky (the male Ouranos) impregnates Earth (the female Gaia) and produces first the hundred-handed monsters and then the Cyclopes. The family pathology then immediately commences, as the father takes the children away from the mother. "Sky tied them (the Cyclopes) up and

2. Exod 32.
3. Camus, *Rebel*.
4. Kelman and Hamilton, *Crimes*.

threw them into Tartarus, a dark and gloomy place in Hades as far from earth as earth is from the sky, and again had children by Earth, the so-called Titans." Such action of course breeds reaction, and Earth repays Sky in spades.

> Grieved at the loss of the children who were thrown into Tartarus, Earth persuaded the Titans to attack their father and gave Cronus a steel sickle . . . Cronus cut off his father's genitals and threw them into the sea . . . Having thus eliminated their Father the Titans brought back their brother who had been hurled to Tartarus and gave the rule to Cronus.[5]

It is not a stretch to say that Zeus, the chief god in the Greek pantheon, has no real interest or compassion for man and indeed may have feared being displaced by man if he empowered him. Zeus thus decides to withhold from man the knowledge of fire, and indeed the means of improving his life. We wish to stress what we have mentioned in chapter 1. Fire was critical to exert some mastery over the environment, in the generation of light and heat necessary for technological and medical advancement. By withholding this knowledge, Zeus, the father god, is keeping man subservient to nature. Prometheus rebels against Zeus in order to help man and does so by stealing fire from Mount Olympus, the home of the gods. Prometheus hides the fire in a hollow fennel stalk and brings it to man, enabling him to gain some autonomy in his fight for survival. Zeus soon learns what has been done and, enraged, creates Pandora (meaning all-gifted), a beautiful but amoral and deceitful creature, as a punishment, and sends her to Epimetheus, the naïve half-brother of the wise Prometheus, along with a jar as a "gift." One day, Pandora decides to open the jar that Zeus sent along with her. The jar contains all the evils in the world, which fly out as soon as Pandora opens it. She closes the lid as quickly as she can, but too late; only hope remains locked in the jar, and unavailable to people.[6]

In early Greek accounts, Prometheus is criticized for upsetting the divine equilibrium. In Hesiod, the story of Prometheus (and, by extension, of Pandora) serves to reinforce the theodicy of Zeus: he is a wise and just ruler of the universe, while Prometheus is to blame for humanity's unenviable existence. Had Prometheus not provoked Zeus's wrath, "you

5. Apollodorus, *Library*, 1.1.4.

6. Hesiod, *Theogony*, lines 533–615; *Works and Days*, lines 53–105.

(man) would easily do work enough in a day to supply you for a full year even without working; soon would you put away your rudder over the smoke, and the fields worked by ox and sturdy mule would run to waste."[7] However, this view is dramatically transposed by the time of the great playwright Aeschylus in the fifth century BCE, who views Prometheus in heroic terms. In *Prometheus Bound*, Prometheus becomes the benefactor of humanity, while every character in the drama (except for Hermes, a virtual stand-in for Zeus) decries the Olympian as a cruel, vicious tyrant.[8] The message in Aeschylus seems clear. Rebellion against a tyrant is essential to gain autonomy!

The following points stand out in this narrative.

1. Zeus is trying to keep man dependent by withholding fire.

2. Prometheus rebels and steals fire to bring man autonomy

3. Zeus, enraged, punishes man by sending the seductive but amoral woman, Pandora.

4. Pandora opens up an urn, unleashing all the evils of the world, making man more dependent again.

2. The Greek Flood Narrative

A similar pattern emerges in a comparison of the Greek narrative of the flood, which probably occurred throughout the Fertile Crescent with the melting of the ice age. Zeus, for no specified reason, sends a great flood to destroy the Bronze race of men. He does not warn an innocent couple, Deucalion (the son of Prometheus) and Pyrrha (the daughter of Pandora and Epimetheus) of the approaching flood, nor does he provide them any means to save themselves.

However, Prometheus once again rebels against Zeus by warning Deucalion of the coming flood and provides instructions on the sly to Deucalion and Pyrrha on how to build a boat. Deucalion and Pyrrha are saved by this boat from the flood. When the flood is over, Deucalion and Pyrrha emerge from the boat. Deucalion sacrifices to Zeus and asks him for a renewal of the human race. Zeus agrees but has the last laugh. He

---

7. Hesiod, *Theogony*, 507–605, especially 545–57; *Works and Days*, 42–105, especially 44–48.

8. Aeschylus, *Prometheus Bound*.

arranges to repopulate the world in a very odd and malevolent way. Men will spring from stones cast by Deucalion and women from stones cast by Pyrrha. His stones become men and hers become women.[9]

Several points stand out in this narrative. First, no real reason is provided for why Zeus orders the flood. He seems to do so arbitrarily. Second, once again, Prometheus must rebel against Zeus to preserve mankind. Thirdly, men and women are perceived as emerging from separate sources, rather than from joint parentage. Zeus repopulates the world through cloning! Deucalion clones men, and Pyrrha women. Finally, there is no guarantee that Zeus will not send another flood if he so chooses.

Several points stand out in this narrative.

1. Zeus orders the flood for no specific reason rather than out of any moral sense.

2. Once again, Prometheus must rebel against Zeus to preserve mankind. This time he steals the blueprint for an ark and gives it to Deucalion and Pyrrha.

3. Thus the father-destroyer and the son-savior are distinct.

4. Finally, Zeus does not promise not to send another flood if he so chooses.

Biblical Narratives

1. The Biblical Creation Narrative

The biblical account of creation is very different. God exists prior to nature and in fact creates the heaven and the earth. "In the beginning God created the heaven and the earth." God himself creates man in his own image as his ultimate handiwork and gives him dominion over the world. He does not want man to be subservient to nature. Rather than withholding fire from man to keep him dependent, Jewish Midrash portrays God as providing the means for Adam to invent fire after his expulsion from Eden because he has compassion for the human beings he has created.[10]

9. Apollodorus, *Library*, 1.7.2.
10. *Midrash Genesis Rabbah* 11:2.

Therefore, man does not need to rebel against God to gain knowledge or autonomy. Instead, autonomy and wisdom are freely given by the biblical God. "The beginning of wisdom is the fear of the Lord."[11]

When the serpent is tempting the first biblical woman with the siren calls of disobedience to gain freedom, the call is superfluous as the biblical God has willingly given freedom to man. Thus, in biblical thinking, eating of the fruit of the tree of knowledge is sinful and indeed foolish, perhaps most of all because it is unnecessary and counterproductive. Wisdom is not seen as located in a fruit, but in awe of God. "The fear of the Lord is the beginning of knowledge."[12] This is not a dictum to keep man ignorant, but rather a declaration that man has God's blessing to gain knowledge and thus does not have to rebel against him to gain it. We might ask if the very idea that knowledge exists in a magical fruit is pagan to the core.

It is the biblical God who has man's interests at heart, not the serpent. Indeed, God does not kill or abandon his creations even after they have disobeyed him. He exiles Adam and his wife from Eden, but makes clothes for them and sets the stage for the birth of their children. Indeed man calls his wife Eve (*Chava* in Hebrew) because she becomes the mother of all living.[13] So the biblical God does not abandon Adam and Eve. Though they lose their personal immortality, they become parents and thus participate in intergenerational continuity.

Although the biblical God is willing to let man and woman have personal immortality, he places the tree that contains the knowledge of sexual reproduction in the garden, but yet forbids them to eat it, lest they die. This, of course, borders on entrapment. The biblical God will not take active personal immortality away from man and woman, but will put a temptation in their path allowing them to choose the forbidden knowledge. This allows them to follow God's commandment to "be fruitful and multiply."[14]

When man and woman choose to eat of this tree, they lose personal immortality but they gain cross-generational immortality, something which is much better for the human being. In other words, they do not immediately die but become parents, in this way they live on in the world

11. Ps 111:10.
12. Prov 1:7.
13. Gen 3:17–21.
14. Gen 1:28.

after their deaths. This reading, of course, turns the famous proclamation of John 3:16[15] in the Christian New Testament on its head. Our analysis suggests the following proclamation: "For God so loved the world that he gave man and woman knowledge of sexual reproduction, so that they may leave the narcissism of personal immortality and enter into the world of cross-generational immortality through parenting and family."

Consider the following analogy. A father tells his son he can live in the father's home as long as he wants to or needs to, but not if he takes a wife and raises a family. The father is telling his son the truth. He is not withholding information like we will argue the Greek oracle does to Oedipus in Corinth. However, when the son chooses to take a wife and raise a family, he must leave the shelter of his father's house and begin his own home. Though his relationship with his father is now different, he still has his father's blessing to "be fruitful and multiply."

The biblical world does value wisdom and autonomy, and in fact it has divine blessing. "Wisdom cries out, she uttereth her voice in the streets."[16] "And you shall teach your children diligently."[17] It is very important in this context not to confuse innocence with ignorance but also not to confuse self-knowledge with sophistry. We must not be afraid of self-knowledge and of knowledge generally, but it must be a healthy and relational knowledge and not a destructive or detached sort of knowledge for its own sake. Wisdom must be rooted in love of God and a positive purpose. "The fear of the Lord is the beginning of knowledge; but the foolish despise wisdom and discipline."[18]

Man need not rebel to gain freedom, as he has already received divine approval to achieve it. Yet when he does rebel, he is not abandoned by God who brought Adam and Eve in the generational continuity of parenthood, only achieved after they were expelled from Eden. One way of looking at this narrative is that the biblical God treats Adam's disobedience as a phase in a dialogue rather than a cause for abandonment. This is much the same stance God took with regard to Jonah in our previous chapter.

Consider the following points.

15. John 3:16: "God so loved the world that he gave his only Son, that everyone who has faith in him, may not die but have eternal life."

16. Ps 1:20.

17. Deut 6:7.

18. Prov 1:7.

1. The biblical God is not trying to keep man subservient but willingly gives him the tools to become autonomous. However, God is calling for a relational rather than a detached knowledge and ethic.

2. The snake offers not freedom, but estrangement from God. He seduces woman to eat of the fruit that ostensibly brings freedom of thought. However the freedom he is offering changes Adam and Eve's relation with God. Yet God foresaw the entire event.

3. Adam's act is not rebellion but disobedience, as he already has freedom in relation to God.

4. The biblical God does not abandon Adam and Eve after their disobedience, but transforms their act as a step in a dialogue. Though Adam and Eve lose personal immortality, they become parents after their expulsion from Eden, thus exchanging personal immortality for intergenerational continuity. They do not live forever themselves, but they do live as links in a generational chain.[19]

2. The Biblical Flood Narrative

The biblical narrative of the flood follows this same pattern.[20] First, the biblical God sends the flood to destroy the men whom he had created because of their wickedness, corruption, and lawlessness. Yet Noah is described as an exception, as a just man and perfect in his generation, and as "walking with God."[21] God himself warns Noah of the coming flood and provides him with an exact blueprint for an ark that will save him. God is rewarding Noah for his obedience. Thus Noah does not need a Promethean figure to rebel against God. God also instructs Noah to bring male and female of each species on board the ark. After the flood ceases, all the living creatures, male and female, come out from the ark and repopulate the earth through their sexual union. Finally, God places a rainbow in the heavens as a sign of his covenant with man that he will not send another flood to destroy man.

A number of points stand out in this narrative.

---

19. The Hebrew phrase *mi dor la dor* (from generation to generation) expresses this thought nicely.

20. Gen 6–9.

21. Gen 6:9.

1. The biblical God brings the flood out of outrage with regard to the immoral behavior of the human beings he has created.

2. God willingly gives Noah the blueprint for the ark because he is a just man who walks with God. In other words, Noah is rewarded for his obedience.

3. Thus the biblical God both brings the flood but also provides the ark to save mankind.

4. The biblical God places a rainbow in the heaven as a promise. He will send no more floods.

A Contemporary Illustration

You find yourself developing a very innovative idea at your workplace. You think it could make a lot of money, and you are thinking that you want to develop and market it on your own. You tell your supervisor about your plans and he advises you not to go out on your own but to work under him to develop the idea for your company. Should you listen to your supervisor or go your own way?

You talk about this with two friends. The first friend urges you not to listen to your supervisor, arguing that your supervisor is trying to block you from going out on your own and is trying to keep you subservient to him. The second friend gives you different advice. He reminds you that your supervisor has always been supportive of you and always tried to aid your advancement.

What will you do? What criteria will you employ to decide whether or not to obey or disobey the advice of your supervisor?

PSYCHO-BIBLICAL GUIDE THREE

Learn how to distinguish a concerned versus a capricious authority. Generally obey the first, but disobey the second. The biblical God first willingly teaches man the means to light a fire, and later when he is planning to send a flood out of moral repugnance for human behavior, he rewards Noah for his obedience and gives him the blueprint to the ark to save the human race. Zeus, in contrast, first withholds fire from man out of personal pique and then sends a flood without giving mankind any means of salvation. Prometheus must rebel against Zeus to save man and he does so twice. First, Prometheus steals fire for man in a fennel stalk, and second he steals the blueprint of the ark and gives it to man.

4

Relating to the Opposite Sex

PSYCHO-BIBLICAL ISSUE FOUR:

How do I know whether or not to listen to my wife/girlfriend? I am afraid she is trying to block my advancements in my career and keep me enmeshed to her. What can I do to be listened to by my husband/ boyfriend? When he doesn't listen to me, I feel disconnected from him.

THE DIFFERENCE BETWEEN THE Greek and biblical accounts of the relationship between men and women is vividly portrayed in a contrast of the story of Prometheus and Pandora with that of Adam and Eve. Pandora is described as a curse and punishment sent by Zeus in retaliation for Prometheus's theft of fire for man. This estrangement continues in the Greek story of the flood and the relationship between Deucalion (the son of Prometheus) and Pyrrha (the daughter of Epimetheus and Pandora). After the flood, new men and women are cloned separately, men from rocks thrown by Deucalion and women from rocks thrown by Pyrrha. This antagonism is expressed in one theory of the derivation of the name "Antigone" as meaning "against" (*anti*) "man" (*gony* referring to male seed or semen) in ancient Greek.

The biblical Eve, in contrast, is described as a blessing to Adam and as a helpmeet (*ezer*) opposite (*kenegdo*) in ancient Hebrew. Eve is "in opposition" to Adam but she is not "against" him. After eating of the fruit of the Tree of Knowledge of Good and Evil, they become aware of their nakedness. Adam names his wife Eve (*Chava* in Hebrew denoting "the mother of all living").[1] At this point, Adam and Eve are expelled from Eden together. Only now does Adam "know" Eve, and she conceives: first Cain, and then Abel, and finally Seth, from whom humankind descends.[2] The union between men and women continues in the biblical account of the flood.[3] New men and women emerge from the sexual union of the sons of Noah and their wives, unlike the separate cloning of men and women, as described in the Greek flood story in the previous chapter.

Greek Narratives

In Plato's *Symposium*, Aristophanes tells a story about how the earliest people were made up of three sexes: men, women, and hermaphrodite circle people—a combination of the first two. These primeval people were so mighty and arrogant that they even thought to ascend Mount Olympus and attack the gods. Zeus decided to slice them in two, not to provide them with companions as in the biblical account, but to humble their pride and also to weaken them and make them more pliable to the gods.[4]

An early woman in the Greek account is Pandora, meaning all-gifted. In the Greek account, as mentioned in chapters 1 and 3, Prometheus steals fire from Mount Olympus, the home of the gods, and, hiding it in a hollow fennel stalk, brings it to man, enabling him to survive. Zeus soon learns what has been done and, enraged, creates Pandora, a beautiful but deceitful creature, as a punishment, and sends her along with a jar as a "gift to Epimetheus," the naïve half-brother of the wise Prometheus. She is amoral if not immoral and described as "a race apart." She is not just seen as "other" but "alien,"[5] a worldview that is expressed in one theory regarding the derivation of the name "Antigone" as meaning "against man."[6]

1. Gen 3.
2. Gen 4.
3. Gen 6:9—10:32.
4. Plato, *Symposium*.
5. Cantz and Kaplan, "Cross-cultural reflections."
6. This destructive and potentially dangerous view is expressed in the modern popular book by John Gray: *Men are from Mars, Women are from Venus.*

One day, Pandora decides to open the jar that Zeus sent along with her. The jar contains all the evils in the world, which fly out as soon as Pandora opens it. She closes the lid as quickly as she can, but too late: only hope remains locked in the jar, unavailable to people.[7] In this Greek account, fire gives man some autonomy, but the beautiful Pandora ruins it all. We should not forget that despite her charm she is described as having the morals of a bitch and is described as being sent as a punishment and an enduring curse to man.

Woman does not simply domesticate man but brings about his ruin, stripping him of any autonomy he may achieve. Woman is seen as the castrator of man and a sexual relationship as a not-so-tender trap and man's undoing.[8] Consider *hystera*, the Greek term for womb from which English words like "hysteria" and "hysterectomy" emerge in our psychiatric and medical vocabulary. The *hystera* is a source of labile and even mercurial affect. No wonder Greek man fears female sexuality! Semonides of Amorgos compares women to sows, vixen, bitches, donkeys, weasels, and monkeys, and says: "No one day goes by from end to end enjoyable, when you have to spend it with your wife."[9] In Greek literature, men and women consistently work against one another, frustrating each other's purpose. Yet avoiding marriage leaves man alone in his old age.[10]

Greek literature portrays woman as, at best, a necessary evil. In Euripides' tragedy *Medea*, the protagonist Jason laments that "it would be better for children to have come into this world by some other means and women never to have existed. Then life would be good."[11] His wife, Medea, strikingly, shares this debased view of women, saying," it would be better to serve in battle three times than bear one child."[12]

Medea's words are also reflected in the *maenads* (frenzied women) of Greek mythology. Described by Euripides in *The Bacchae,* as well as in other sources, *maenads* were ordinary women who would leave their homes for orgiastic dancing in the forests. There they would run around bare-breasted and suckle animal cubs; and they would tear animals apart

---

7. Hesiod, *Works and Days*, lines 47–104, and *Theogony*, lines 521–602.

8. Apollodorus, *Library,* 1.

9. Semonides of Amorgos, 11.

10. Hesiod, *Theogony,* lines 600–610.

11. Euripides, *Medea* , lines 573–75.

12. Ibid., 244–51.

(*sparagmos* in Greek) and eat them raw (*omaphagia*). In the Euripides play, Agave tears off the head of her son Pentheus when she encounters him during this possessed state.[13]

When the woman is portrayed as a castrator of man, a sexual relationship is seen as a sinister rather than tender trap—and the origin of man's undoing. This is also the pattern of the Olympian story of creation. Gaia, the earth goddess, colludes with her son, Cronus, to castrate her husband and his father, Ouranos, the sky god, as Ouranos approaches her for intercourse. No wonder Greek men feared female sexuality! Woman is dangerous, and man runs the risk of losing his manhood in a sexual relationship with her. It is no far stretch to suggest that fear of female sexuality contributed to the encouragement of the Greek male's interest in young boys and barely pubescent girls.[14] Indeed, one of the few acceptable female figures in classical Greece is Athena, the virgin goddess. Born from Zeus's head, she carries her *aegis* (shield) topped with a Medusa head, and she thus appears to remove herself from this dangerous female sexuality.

Another striking estrangement between men and women emerges in the Greek flood narrative discussed in chapter 3. What is critical in this chapter on men and women is the description of how the world becomes repopulated after the flood. When the flood is over, Deucalion and Pyrrha emerge from the boat. Deucalion sacrifices to Zeus and asks him for a renewal of the human race. Zeus agrees but has the last laugh. He arranges to repopulate the world in a very odd and malevolent way. Men will spring from stones cast by Deucalion and women from stones cast by Pyrrha. His stones become men and hers become women.[15],

The following points stand out in these narratives.

1. Zeus sends Pandora as a punishment to man because Prometheus has stolen fire for him. Thus woman is portrayed as a punishment for man's attempts to become autonomous.

---

13. Euripides, *Bacchae*.

14. Slater, *Glory of Hera*, 4; Gundlach and Riess, "Identity."

15. Apollodorus, *Library*, 1.7.2. To be sure, a subsequent account in Apollodorus does suggest a sexual union between Deucalion and Pyrrha. "Deucalion had children by Pyrrha, first, Helen . . . second, Amphicytron, and third, a daughter, Potogenia" (Apollodorus, *Library*, 1.7.3). Nevertheless, the account of separate cloning seems highly significant in a society as misogynistic as ancient Greece in that it continues the view of Pandora and woman as a "race apart."

2. Pandora is seductive but amoral and is described as a "race apart."

3. Pandora opens up an urn, unleashing all the evils of the world, making man more dependent again. Woman's womb (*hystera*) is seen as the source of labile, untrustworthy emotion (*hysteria*).

4. After the flood, the world is repopulated through separate cloning, Deucalion throwing stones over his shoulder to become men and Pyrrha throwing stones over her shoulder to become women.

Biblical Narratives

The creation of people in Genesis is different. It is the beautiful culmination of six days of creation by a benevolent and all-wise God. With all Adam's achievements, he is very alone. God sees that it is not good for a man to be alone, so according to the second creation story in Genesis, he puts Adam into a deep sleep and separates part of his body, thus dividing the original human into two beings, a man and a woman. Eve is created as a "helpmeet opposite" (*ezer kenegdo*[16] in biblical Hebrew) to man, a part of a complete human relationship, rather than as a curse.

Biblical narratives basically portray men and women as different, but in basic harmony.[17] Eve is sent as a blessing and partner, not as punishment. Eve is misled by the serpent into seeing God's prohibition to eat of the Tree of Knowledge as an attempt to enslave her and Adam rather than to ensure that they use their abilities to carry out their roles in God's creation. Adam and Eve do not suddenly gain in wisdom, for wisdom is not contained in a magical fruit. What they do learn is that they are naked, and perhaps they gain the sexual knowledge of human reproduction.

Adam and Eve disobey God and are sent out from Eden, and they will no longer live indefinitely, but they will become parents. They will have to struggle and work hard, but can still have wonderful lives. The woman is told she will bear children in pain, but Adam also gives her the name Eve (Hebrew: *Chava)* meaning "mother of life." Adam in turn will obtain food through the sweat of his brow. Adam and Eve are now aware of their nakedness, but God signals his recognition and empathy in their new situation by giving them warm and pleasant garments to cover them.

16. Gen 2:18.
17. Gen 1–4.

Certainly, the biblical message in all this is far different from the message of the Greek world. Attachment is not seen as inconsistent with freedom, nor woman as a block to man's autonomy. Nor are sexual relations with a woman to be feared by man. In the biblical view there is no stigma attached to women, and sexual love is a blessing. When Genesis refers to Adam "knowing" Eve, it refers to both a physical and a spiritual knowing. The Hebrew term for womb is *rehem*, which is connected to the Hebrew word *rahamim*, meaning mercy or compassion, and a term used to describe God himself. Anything but unstable in this view, woman provides a secure base for human development.

The helpmeet opposite can concur with her husband's decision or she can oppose it, if she judges him to be in error. However, she does this in a supportive rather than a destructive way, with the aim of preserving and fulfilling the divine purpose of the family. A helpmeet opposite can oppose her husband when he is wrong, and indeed must oppose him in such a circumstance. But she must do this in a helpful rather than antagonistic manner.[18]

Throughout the Hebrew Bible, women are typically portrayed as figures with great moral strength who express their humanity in areas of human relations and in service before God. Women like Sarah and Rebecca play major roles in carrying out the divine mission of building a new faith and nation based on monotheism, wisdom, and love. To carry out this mission, a woman may need to do many things, beginning with giving support as wife and mother and going on to the wide range of emotional, economic, and social activities attributed to the "woman of valor" in Proverbs 31. In Mark Twain's story "Adam's Diary," Adam says that he treasured Eve more and more as time went on, for he learned that, though they had been sent out of the garden, wherever she was was Eden for him.[19]

The conclusion of the biblical flood story also highlights the essential harmony between man and woman. On instructions from the biblical God, Noah has gathered male and female of all species onto the ark. After the flood has ceased, all the living creatures, male and female, come out from the ark and repopulate the earth through their sexual union, not through separate cloning as in the Greek flood account.

18. Schwartz and Kaplan, *Fruit*.

19. Twain, *Diaries*.

The biblical view of woman may be summarized as follows.

1. The biblical God sends woman as a "helpmeet opposite" to Adam so he should not be alone.

2. Woman is made of the same substance as Adam, in one story being made as the same time as man, and in the second, made out of his rib.

3. Although Eve eats of the fruit of the forbidden tree and convinces Adam to do likewise, God does not kill them, and they become joint parents together after their expulsion from Eden. Although they will no longer live eternally themselves, they will now become links in the intergenerational chain. Woman's womb (*rehem*) is seen as the source of solid emotion and compassion (*rahamim*).

4. After the flood, males and females repopulate the world through their sexual union.

A Contemporary Illustration

Jeff is an Assistant Professor in Biochemistry at a Midwestern state university and has been married for several years to Carol. Their relationship is very intense, but Jeff sometimes feels that Carol is overly demanding. Carol, in turn, feels that Jeff is overly preoccupied with his work, does not pay enough attention to her or their marriage, and still behaves like a single man. She wishes he would leave the university and take a higher paying job in a private research company. She wants to stop working and start a family. Jeff, on the other hand, is heavily invested in his original research and wants very much to gain tenure.

Jeff receives an invitation to take a leave from the university to take a prestigious post-doctoral fellowship with a major figure in his field. Though the fellowship would involve a temporary reduction in salary, he believes this fellowship will propel his career upward, and land him a more prestigious and even higher paying job down the road. He is very happy and rushes home excitedly to tell Carol his wonderful news. However, Carol is not at all happy. She asks him not to take this fellowship, but instead to think about getting a higher paying job in the private sphere so she can stop working and they can begin a family.

This is not an uncommon problem. Should Jeff listen to Carol or not? Should he agree to her request or should he pursue what he thinks is right. Are Carol's motives selfish like Pandora or are they acts of a true partner like Eve? How can Carol get Jeff to listen to her?

PSYCHO-BIBLICAL GUIDE FOUR

Judge if your wife/girlfriend is behaving like Eve or Pandora. Remember, part of the way she behaves will be a function of the way in which you are treating her. Remember the desired state is to treat your significant other as a blessing and a partner (Eve) rather than as a punishment and adversary (Pandora). See if your husband/boyfriend listens to you or not. Part of the way he reacts will depend on how you express yourself to him.

5

Relating to a Son

**PSYCHO-BIBLICAL ISSUE FIVE
(PRIMARILY TO A FATHER):**

*How should I relate to my adolescent son? I am afraid that when he
grows up he will surpass me, have no respect for me, and make me
irrelevant.*

GREEK MYTHOLOGY PORTRAYS FATHERS and sons in a bitter rivalry, with
sons seen as a threat to their fathers' position and the fathers as a block to
their sons' development. Sons must not surpass their fathers or threaten
their position in any way, and it is perfectly legitimate for fathers to practice infant exposure. Cronus eats his children, and Zeus begets and aban-
dons illegitimate children all over the earth. The son in this system has no
real right to live. In the Roman conception of *patria potestas*, the father
holds the power of infant exposure over his son.

The biblical father-son relationship is generally diametrically different. Parental aggression toward children, which so dominates classical
Greek thought and Freudian psychology, has no formal place in biblical
or rabbinic thought. Indeed, biblical narratives take it as natural that a
father will be happy if his child surpasses him. The father is not the owner
of his son as with the Roman *patria potestas,* nor does he hold the power
of infant exposure. One of the most significant themes in the rabbinic

literature is the command to the father to teach his children thoroughly.[1] The father's identity is not threatened by the son; he wants to see his son develop and surpass him.

Greek Narratives

Two mythical father-son relationships exemplify the Greek pattern very well: (1) Creon and his son Haemon, and (2) the famous narrative of Laius and Oedipus.

1. Creon and Haemon

The relationship between Creon and Haemon in Sophocles' *Antigone* portrays Creon as an impossible father who puts his son Haemon in an impossible position. Will Haemon obey his father and consign his fiancée, Antigone, buried alive, to her doom, or will he oppose his father in an attempt to save her?

Creon sees Haemon's attempt to express his own point of view as disloyalty to the family agenda, and thus his first words are to question whether Haemon will remain loyal to him. Haemon responds mildly at first, submitting to his father's authority, but then he attempts to defend Antigone to his father. Creon responds: "Men of my age, are we indeed to be schooled by men of his?"[2] The exchange between father and son becomes quite bitter: Haemon demands that his father judge him by his merits rather than his years, and Creon responds by accusing Haemon of shamelessly feuding with his father. Creon emphasizes his control and power by introducing the issue of Haemon's death: "Thou canst never marry on this side of the grave." Haemon's response contains a clear suicidal threat: "Then she must die, and in her deeds, destroy another."[3] Creon calls his son's bluff, and Haemon raises the ante violently. When Creon interrupts Haemon's mourning for the now-dead Antigone, Haemon reacts violently: first, he tries unsuccessfully to kill his father, and then he kills himself.

---

1. Deut 6:7; *b. Kiddushin* 30a.
2. Sophocles, *Antigone,* lines 727–28.
3. Ibid., 750–51.

2. Laius and Oedipus

The most widely known and paradigmatic example of the Greek mytho-
logical father-son relationship is of course that of Laius and Oedipus as
portrayed in Sophocles' great tragedy, *Oedipus Rex*. It can be summarized
as follows.

> King Laius of Thebes was warned by an oracle that there was
> danger to his throne and life if his son, newborn, should reach
> man's estate. He, therefore, committed the child to a herdsman
> with order for its destruction. The herdsman, after piercing the
> infant's feet, gave him to a fellow-shepherd, who carried him to
> King Polybus of Corinth and his queen, by whom he was adopted
> and called Oedipus, or swollen-foot.
>
> Many years later, Oedipus, learning from an Oracle that he was
> destined to be the death of his father, left the realm of his reputed
> sire, Polybus. It happened, however, that Laius was then driving to
> Delphi, accompanied only by one attendant. In a narrow road he
> met Oedipus. A quarrel broke out, and Oedipus slew both Laius
> and his attendant. Shortly after this event, Oedipus saved Thebes
> from the sphinx, a monster, part woman, part lion and part eagle,
> which had been devouring all who could not guess her riddle[4] . . .
> In gratitude for their deliverance, the Thebans made Oedipus their
> King, giving him marriage to their queen, his mother.[5]

The Oedipus legend fits into a primary type of Greek myth, which
we have discussed in chapter 1. Cronus, the youngest son of Ouranos,
with the help of his mother, Gaia, rose against his father, castrating and
dethroning him. Cronus, in turn, swallowed his own children as soon
as they were born to avoid being supplanted by them. However, Zeus,
his youngest son, survived, overpowering Cronus with the help of his
mother, Rhea, and became king. Zeus, in turn, devoured his wife with the
embryo in her womb.[6] The mother may be seen as providing the "keys to
the kingdom" rather than as exclusively an object of sexual desire, and the
father is motivated to destroy the son to keep his own power position. His

4. An interesting side-note is the nature of the Sphinx's riddle: "What walks on four
legs in the morning, two legs in the afternoon, and three legs in the evening." When
Oedipus answers "man," he is implicitly accepting a curvilinear or decremental view of
aging where the older adult is seen like an infant, which may contribute to the blurring of
the intergenerational boundaries between himself and his mother-wife, Jocasta.

5. Gayley, *Myths,* 261–64; Sophocles, *Oedipus Rex*, lines 369–422.

6. Apollodorus, *Library,* 1.1.4.

threat of castration is similarly motivated—to neutralize the son's threat of displacement.[7]

The family pattern emerging from these stories seems self-evident. First, husband and wife are estranged from each other. The husband is disengaged and wife is enmeshing. Family triangulation occurs, pitting mother and son against father. Moreover, the pattern seems a natural consequence of creation, and is destined to repeat itself cyclically throughout the generations (see Freud's historical reconstruction in *Totem and Taboo* of primordial groups dominated by a strong male who threatened to kill, castrate, or drive out sons trying to steal his women. The sons collectively overcame, murdered, and ingested the father, and an implicit social contract emerged to avoid further conflict: the taboo of incest and the law requiring exogamy).[8]

The traditional psychoanalytic explanation of resolution of the Oedipus Complex is incomplete and ambivalent at best. In this unresolved state the Greek husband-father is disengaged from and deprecating to his wife and terrified of absorption by her. He also fears displacement by his son who in turn sees his father as a block to his development. The wife-mother is enmeshed. She envies her husband and fears he will abandon her. She attempts to control and seduce her son. The son is anomically

---

7. Kohut, "Introspection, empathy," 404–5. Kohut has pointed to an exception to this rule: the loyalty of Telemachus to his absent father Odysseus. Graves (*Myths*, 279) cites Hyginus (Fabulae, 95) in pointing to Odysseus's saving of his infant son Telemachus when Palamedes has thrown him in front of Odysseus's plow. Nevertheless, Odysseus goes to fight in the Trojan War and is absent all during Telemachus's formative years. Indeed in the first four books of Homer's *The Odyssey*, Telemachus is portrayed as trying to gain knowledge of his father. Further, this entire story may be an anomaly that proves the rule, as the loyalty of Penelope, the wife of the absent Odysseus, in rejecting would-be suitors is quite unlike the more typical resentment exhibited by Greek women towards their husbands (e.g., Clytemnestra, Medea, and Deineira). Another seeming exception is that of Orestes' loyalty to his slain father Agamemnon. Here there is no love lost between Orestes' mother Clytemnestra and her husband Agamemnon (she in fact has participated in his slaying). In works by the three great Greek tragedians, Orestes kills his mother Clytemnestra to avenge her slaying his father (Aeschylus, *The Choephori*; Sophocles, *Electra*; Euripides, *Electra*). One must wonder, however, given Agamemnon's brutal insensitivity in his treatment of his wife Clytemnestra and his callous sacrificing of his daughter Iphigenia, how Agamemnon would have acted towards Orestes had he lived. Further, the Aeschylus version of this tragedy suggests that Orestes may be motivated by profound Greek religious factors regarding the elimination of pollutants rather than love for his father Agamemnon per se.

8. Freud, *Totem and Taboo*.

split between disengagement and enmeshment, wanting to drive out and displace his father and possess his mother.

Classic psychoanalytic thinking only allows for an ambivalent resolution. The father counters his son's threat of displacement by threatening to castrate him. This threat serves to neutralize rather than resolve the son's desire to displace his father, resulting in a cold peace and a mutual standoffishness between father and son. The son still sees his father as a block; the father, in turn, continues to see his son as a threat.

The husband-wife relationship remains unchanged, with the husband still deprecating his wife and the wife still envying her husband. The mother will still try to seduce her son but the son has given up his desire to possess his mother, now fearing incorporation by her. The son has displaced his fear of castration from his father to his mother. This ambivalent neutralization of the Oedipal dilemma leaves the son in a disengaged position with both his father and mother.

As the son's superego is introjected in this process,[9] it reflects a detached and isolated quality. In the process of identifying with his father, the son displaces his fear of castration onto his mother, thus laying the foundation for a suspicion and fear of women.[10] Furthermore, this pathology, without corrective therapy, is likely to reproduce itself from generation to generation. The disengaged son will himself grow up to be a disengaged father. If he marries an enmeshed intrusive woman, this pattern will be repeated in the next generation.

These Greek narratives can be seen to share a number of elements.

1. The father is afraid that his son will attempt to displace or even kill him and marry his mother should he reach man's estate.

2. The mother sometimes provides the son assistance in his rebellion, largely because of her husband's ill treatment of her.

3. To retain his position, the father attempts to destroy or block his son. In the psychoanalytic resolution, the father threatens to castrate the son.

---

9. Freud, *Ego and Id*; "Organizations"; "Dissolution."

10. See Bruno Bettelheim's discussion of the *vagina dentata* image (i.e., the castrating and devouring vagina with teeth) in the Liberian Poro society (Bettelheim, *Symbolic Wounds*, 115). Also see Karl Abraham's report of a modern western male patient who likened the vagina to the jaws of a crocodile (Abraham, *Selected Papers*, 463).

4. To avoid this, the son reaches a cold peace with his father, giving up his overt attempts to displace his father and possess his mother, but still viewing him as a block to his own development. As the introjection of the Freudian superego occurs as a function of the resolution of the Oedipus Complex, the son's morality is based on fear and appears stiff and formal.

Biblical Narratives

The very idea that the son is a threat to a father rather than an extension of him in the future is very foreign to the biblical worldview. The father knows that the son is not motivated to displace him because the son knows that he will inherit from him. The father's identity is not threatened by the son. Indeed, he wants to see his son develop and surpass him and is commanded to teach him thoroughly.[11] A father sees himself as a link in the generational chain, carrying on his own father's legacy and passing it on to his son. Two biblical father-son relationships exemplify this pattern very well: (1) Jacob and his sons, and (2) the famous *Akedah* narrative of Abraham and Isaac.

1. Jacob and His Sons

Consider first the story of Jacob blessing his sons. The full story will discussed at great length in chapter 7 on relating to siblings. For our purposes here, it suffices to emphasize that Jacob, now a very old man, comes to Egypt, renews his relationship with Joseph, and makes certain that Joseph's sons, Ephraim and Manasseh, even though born in Egypt, are included within the family and are full recipients of its teachings and traditions. Finally, Jacob blesses his sons in terms of each one's unique strengths and weaknesses, affirming each as an individual personality and recognizing his unique role and creativity in the covenant. "All these are the twelve tribes of Israel, and this is what their father spoke to them. And he blessed them; he blessed each one according to his own blessing."[12]

---

11. Deut 6:7; *b. Kiddushin* 30a.
12. Gen 49:28.

2. Abraham and Isaac

Over fifty years ago, the visionary Jewish psychiatrist Erich Wellisch seized on the paradigmatic story of Abraham and Isaac (the *Akedah* or "binding") as a narrative reflecting this biblical conception of father-son relations. For Wellisch, the *Akedah* represents not a sacrifice story but a story to forbid and end child sacrifice and offers a new approach to psychiatry. The core of his argument is that the *Akedah* narrative suggests an unambivalent resolution of the father-son relationship that is based on a covenant of love and shared purpose between parent and child rather than a compromise between the parental wish to possess the possess the child completely or even to kill him and the desire not to do so.[13]

Wellisch's argument requires a fuller understanding of the relationship between God, Abraham, and Isaac, and the outworking of the covenant between them. Abram's relationship with God begins when God is portrayed as telling him (Abram) to leave his father Terah's house and his pagan gods.[14]

Abram's relationship with God develops. Sarai is barren and arranges for Abram (now named Abraham) to have a son, Ishmael, with her handmaiden, Hagar.[15] Sarai is renamed Sarah and is given the blessing of a son, Isaac, despite her advanced age of ninety years. God will continue the covenant with Isaac rather than Ishmael, whom he will bless but not give his covenant.[16] Sarah ultimately gives birth to Isaac and Abraham reluctantly sends Ishmael away at Sarah's request after Ishmael makes sport at Isaac's weaning.[17]

After all these events, we are confronted with the narrative of the *Akedah* text itself. First, God calls upon Abraham to offer his son Isaac, who, God acknowledges, is Abraham's only son whom he loves, as a sacrifice.[18] Secondly, Abraham seems prepared to go through with the sacrifice, never fully giving up hope that God will transform his command so that Isaac might be saved. Further, Isaac trusts in his father, despite his questioning with regard to the absence of a burnt offering.[19] Finally, God

13. Wellisch, *Isaac and Oedipus*, 3–4, 79, 89.
14. Gen 12:1–3.
15. Gen 17:5.
16. Gen 17:20–21.
17. Gen 21:8–11.
18. Gen 22:2.
19. Gen 22:6–8.

does relent, sending an angel at the last moment to command Abraham not to sacrifice Isaac: "Lay not thine hand upon the lad."[20]

The concretization of the covenant between father and son and Wellisch's "instinct modification" is symbolized by circumcision of the male foreskin at the age of eight days: "And God said unto Abraham . . . 'And ye shall be circumcised in the flesh of your foreskin: and it shall be token of a covenant betwixt me and you.'"[21]

Circumcision has often been viewed in psychoanalytic thinking as symbolic castration. However, it is better viewed as a sanctified, non-injurious substitute linked to the biblical covenant itself between God and Israel (*b'rit ha-milah*), which actually transforms the primordial fear on the part of the son into his very assurance that the father's own interests lie in the son's being fit to carry on the covenant.

To summarize, the biblical family has a purpose, the passing down of a covenant. The father's covenant with his son in the *Akedah* narrative is symbolized by non-injurious circumcision that transforms in one fell swoop the social contract emerging from the balance of terror between the father's fear of displacement and the son's fear of castration into an intergenerational bond wherein each generation has a vested interest in the well-being of the other. The father knows the son does not need to displace him. The son is aware that the father could have castrated him but chose not to. The son wants a teacher, the father wants an heir.[22]

The Akedah Motif within which the son develops, as expressed in circumcision, can transform the above relationships and resolve unambivalently the Oedipus Complex. The biblical family has a purpose. The husband honors and loves his wife. She in turn respects and loves her husband. The father does not fear displacement by the son and is thus free to protect and instruct him. The mother does not act seductively to her son or attempt to triangulate with him against her husband. She instead nurtures him in an attempt to develop his personality. The biblical matriarch serves in a mediating role between father and son, in passing down the covenant to the most-suited heir. The son does not desire to possess his mother or displace his father.[23] Instead he accepts protection and

20. Gen 22:9–12.

21. Gen 17:9–11.

22. Kaplan, "Isaac and Oedipus: reexamination"; Kaplan, "Isaac and Oedipus: alternative view."

23. A seeming exception to this pattern is the rebellion of Absalom against his father

nurturance from his parents and learns from them. It is this assurance of paternal protection that allows the son to develop at his own pace in a healthy way. The son's introjection of his superego is based not on fear but on love and his moral conscience will be engaged rather than disengaged. The son will not be standoffish but able to go into an adult relationship as a full personality who is not afraid to love.

This view is expressed succinctly in the Book of Malachi in the Hebrew Bible:

> And He shall turn the heart of the fathers to the children,
> And the heart of the children to their fathers;
> Lest I smite the land with utter destruction.[24]

These narratives can be seen to share a number of elements.

1. The father wants his son to inherit from him and even surpass him.

2. The mother participates in this process, even at times helping to choose the most suitable heir.

3. The father participates in the biblical ritual of covenantal circumcision (*b'rit ha-milah*) transforming the fear of castration into a rite of inheritance. The father becomes the teacher, the son the heir.

4. As a result the son arrives at a covenantal relationship with his father, joining him in a passing down of the biblical covenant. As the introjection of this biblical superego occurs out of a covenantal love, the son's morality is based on compassion and is flexible rather than stiff and rigid.

David to become King of Israel (2 Sam 15:1—18:32), but even here, despite all the mischief that Ahitophel can do (2 Sam 16:16—17:23), David never stops loving Absalom his son, grieving mightily for him when he hears of his death (2 Sam 19:1–9). Upon hearing of his rebellious son's death, David weeps and laments, "My son, Absalom. My son, my son, Absalom! Would that I had died in your stead" (2 Sam 19:1), and later he cries in a loud voice, "Absalom! Absalom! my son, my son" (2 Sam 19:5). These words became the title of a profound novel by the great American novelist William Faulkner (Faulkner, *Absalom, Absalom!*). See the excellent interpretation of this episode by Robert Alter (*David Story*, 290–313). Adonijah, another son of David also strives to gain David's throne. This attempt, however, only occurs at the end of David's life and is an example of sibling rivalry against Adonijah's half-brother Solomon, rather than a rebellion against David per se. "And Adonijah son of Haggith was giving himself airs, saying, 'I *shall be* king'" (1 Kgs 1:1—2:45).

24. Mal 3:24.

Contemporary Illustrations

The 2007 movie *There Will Be Blood*[25] portrays a destructive Oedipal father-son relationship. In 1902, Daniel Plainview, a mineral prospector, played brilliantly by Daniel Day Lewis, discovers oil and establishes a small drilling company. Following the death of one of his workers in an accident, Plainview adopts the man's orphaned son (his mother nowhere to be found). The boy, whom he names H. W., becomes his nominal business "partner."

Nine years later, Plainview is approached by Paul Sunday, who tells him about the oil deposit under his family's property in Little Boston, California. Plainview maneuvers to buy the farm at a bargain price. Oil production begins. Later, an on-site accident kills a worker, and later still, a large explosion robs H. W. of his hearing.

In 1927, a much older H. W. marries his childhood sweetheart, Mary Sunday. By this time his father, now alcoholic but extremely wealthy, is living in a mansion with only a servant for company. H. W. asks his father (through an interpreter) to dissolve their partnership so he can establish his own business. Plainview feels betrayed and tells H. W. he will regret his behavior. H. W. tries to explain to his father that he is not being disloyal to him but wants to develop his own identity and leaves open the possibility of working with him again. Rather than encouraging H. W. and wanting him to succeed, Plainview views his son as his "competitor." Plainview mocks his son's deafness and tells him of his true origins, shouting at him that he is a "bastard in a basket," driving H. W. away. H. W. leaves for good, with no regrets, expressing relief that he is not biologically related to Plainview.

Tim Burton's 2003 movie *Big Fish*[26] presents a very different example of a father-son relationship. Albert Finney plays Edward Bloom, a former travelling salesman from the Southern United States with a gift for storytelling, now confined to his deathbed. Bloom's estranged son Will, a journalist, attempts to mend their relationship as his dying father relates tall tales of his eventful life as a young adult, played by Ewan McGregor. Bloom has told the same tale many times over the years: on the day Will was born, he (Bloom) was out catching an enormous uncatchable fish, using his wedding ring as bait. Will is annoyed, explaining to his wife

25. Anderson, *There Will Be Blood*.
26. Burton, *Big Fish*.

Joséphine that because his father never told the straight truth about anything, he felt unable to trust him. He is troubled to think that he might have a similarly difficult relationship with his future children. Will's relationship with his father becomes so strained that they do not talk for three years. But when his father's health starts to fail, Will and the now pregnant Joséphine return to Alabama. On the plane, Will recalls his father's tale of how he braved a swamp as a child, and met a witch who showed him his death in her glass eye, and met too a huge twelve-foot-tall giant named Karl, an itinerant poet named Norther Winslow, and conjoint twins named Ping and Jing. With this knowledge, Edward knew there were no odds he could not face. Still unimpressed by his father's stories, Will demanded to know the truth, but Edward explained that he is who he is: a storyteller.

Now Will is informed his father had a stroke and is at the hospital. He goes to visit him there and finds him only partly conscious, and unable to speak at length. Since Edward can no longer tell stories, he asks Will to tell him the story of how it all ends. Will tells his dying father a story encapsulating all of his father's "tall tales," which he now understands in a different, more human, light. In Will's story, Edward rises miraculously from his deathbed, and together with his son and the help of his wife, escapes from the hospital. They go to the river where everyone in Edward's life appears to bid him goodbye. Will carries his father into the river where he becomes what he always had been, a very big fish, and the fish swims away. The film then switches back to the actual hospital bed. Edward dies, knowing his son finally understands his love of storytelling, and him.

At the funeral, Will sees many of his father's more unusual friends, including the witch, Karl, Ping and Jing, and Norther Winslow. Will realizes that his father's stories were true, only exaggerated, making Karl a giant (he is, in fact, seven feet six inches) and making Ping and Jing conjoined when they are merely twins. When his own son is born, Will passes on his father's stories, remarking that his father became his stories, allowing him to live forever. This, of course, is the biblical pattern of father-son relations.

~ ~ ~

PSYCHO-BIBLICAL GUIDE FIVE

Empower your son and do not block him. The biblical God makes a covenant with both Abraham and Isaac. Thus Abraham has a vested interest in seeing Isaac succeed and indeed develop fully, even if that means surpassing Abraham. Laius, in contrast, hears from an oracle that his son Oedipus, when he grows into manhood, will kill him and marry his wife. Thus Laius attempts to kill Oedipus. Learn how to support your son and encourage him to succeed to the utmost of his abilities. Do not be afraid he will surpass you and displace you, but encourage him to surpass you if he can. You are a link in a chain of generations.

6

Relating to a Daughter

**PSYCHO-BIBLICAL ISSUE SIX
(PRIMARILY TO A MOTHER):**

How should I relate to my adolescent daughter? I am afraid she will abandon me if she has a life of her own.

THE BIBLICAL STORY OF Ruth provides an alternative to the Greek legend of Electra for understanding the relationship between mothers and daughters. The Ruth narrative suggests an unambivalent resolution of the mother-daughter relationship that is based on a covenant of love and shared purpose between mother and daughter (actually the most problematic relationship of mother-in-law and daughter-in-law). The Greek narrative of Clytemnestra and Electra portrays a vicious and conflictual relationship between mother and daughter, in which mother and daughter viciously attack each other.

Greek Narratives

Although the basic relationship between mother and daughter is very close in the Greek literary tradition, it is tainted by a potentially suicidal lack of genuine self-esteem. Woman is seen as the mysterious "other," closely associated with the devouring earth. This "otherness" is implied in the creation of Pandora as a curse to man, rather than as a suitable helper and a source of life. Her otherness implies alienness rather than simply difference and complementarity.[1] Woman's alien nature is perhaps most clearly expressed in taboos regarding the uncleanness of her menstrual blood. Taboos about menstruation lead to envy of the male[2] and the daughter's willingness to abandon the mother and look to her father.

1. Hecuba and Polyxena

Before we turn to the paradigmatic account of Electra, let us consider the mother-daughter relationship of Hecuba and Polyxena that is described in Euripides' tragedy *Hecuba*. Hecuba, the brave widow of King Priam of Troy, is a captive of the Greeks. Her first speech reveals the depths of her own despair and distaste for life: "Woe, woe is me! What champion have I? Sons, and city—where are they? Aged Creon is no more; no more my children now. Which way am I to go . . . Ye have made an end, an utter end of me; life on earth has no more charm for me."[3]

When Odysseus informs them that Polyxena will be sacrificed to the ghost of Achilles, Hecuba's own emotional structure crumbles so badly that she cannot function as a mother. When Polyxena attempts to talk to her mother about her impending disaster, Hecuba is unable to concentrate on anything but her own problems.

Polyxena understandably bemoans her fate: "Unwedded I depart, never having tasted the married joys that were my due!" Yet Hecuba seems to compete with her as to who is most miserable: "Tell them of all women I am most miserable."[4] Hecuba is without hope. She has earlier expressed this fatalism to her daughter: "Alas, my daughter! . . . Woe for the life! Ah my daughter, a luckless mother's child."[5] Milton Faber has offered a radical interpretation that Hecuba's own paralyzing depression and inability to show a full empathy pushes Polyxena toward suicide.[6]

1. Cantz and Kaplan, "Cross-cultural reflections."
2. Cf. Stephens, *Oedipus Complex*. In a cross-cultural study, Stephens reports a relationship between indices of castration anxiety and the severity of menstrual taboos.
3. Euripides, *Hecuba*, lines 163–70.
4. Ibid., 416, 424.
5. Ibid., 179–85.
6. Faber, *Suicide and Tragedy*, 117.

2. Clytemnestra and Electra

Let us now turn to the paradigmatic Greek mother-daughter relationship, that of Clytemnestra and Electra, the basis for Jung's "Electra Complex."[7] In his play *Electra*, Euripides depicts Electra, daughter of Agamemnon, as waiting for years, completely obsessed by plans for the return of her brother Orestes to wreak revenge on their mother, Clytemnestra, for the murder of their father, Agamemnon. Plotting to murder Clytemnestra, Electra tells her mother that she has just given birth. When Clytemnestra arrives, Electra accuses her mother of cuckolding Agamemnon.[8]

Clytemnestra's response to Electra stresses the preference of the daughter for her father over her mother: "Daughter, 'twas ever thy nature to love thy father."[9] Although Electra participates in the murder of her mother rather than of herself, she displays her essential feeling of debasement as a woman: "Ah me! Alas! And whither can I go? . . . What husband will accept me as his bride?"[10]

The place of the daughter in the classical Greek family is tenuous. She idealizes her father because she needs him. At the same time, he ignores, rejects, or even sacrifices her, as does Agamemnon his other daughter, Iphigenia. Her mother may find it difficult to see her as an independent being. The daughter is thus caught between rejection and enmeshment, and her shaky self-esteem is further diminished by her mother in the latter's attempt to bind her.

The Electra Complex, based on the story of Electra summarized above, is a term proposed by Jung.[11] Freud rejects Jung's use of the term as inaccurate and insists that strictly speaking the Oedipus Complex refers only to males.[12] It denotes the ambivalent desire of the daughter to abandon her mother and possess her father. It is neutralized through the daughter's giving up her father as a sexual object and identifying with her mother. The daughter's resolution in the Freudian view is not complete as she has already been castrated and because of the remaining penis envy

---

7. Jung, *Freud and Psychoanalysis*, 347–48.
8. Euripides, *Electra*, lines 188, 1067–83.
9. Ibid., 1102.
10. Ibid., 1198–1200.
11. Jung, *Freud and Psychoanalysis*, 347–48.
12. Freud, *Three Essays*, 375.

she feels toward her father. It ultimately becomes resolved through her giving birth to a child.[13]

I suggest that a missing dynamic in this process is "shame of menstruation" elicited in the daughter by the mother as a means of neutralizing the mother's own fear of abandonment. There is no question that in many cultures menstrual shame has led to women feeling impure and envious of males.[14] This would explain a daughter's willingness to abandon the mother and to look to her father. Penis envy may be a result rather than a cause of this process.

The mother's defense in this regard may be to lower her daughter's self-esteem by eliciting even further shame about the latter's menstruation and femininity, to make it risky for the daughter fully to abandon the mother lest she herself wind up totally alone—without either mother or father. Such action on the part of the mother results in her daughter accentuating the negative feelings she already has about herself. Attachment between the Greek mother and daughter is thus potentially permeated with a negative symbiotic quality, leaving the daughter unable to cope in a healthy way with life stresses.

Let us summarize these patterns. The Greek wife-mother is enmeshed and envies her husband, yet is terrified of abandonment by him. The mother also fears abandonment by her daughter. The Greek husband-father, in contrast, is disengaged, deprecating his wife and terrified of absorption by her. He is willing to abandon, expose, or sacrifice his daughter. This, of course, evokes the classic Electra Complex for the anomic daughter who is eager to abandon her mother in her idealization of her father.

We have argued above that psychoanalytic thinking fails to provide a satisfactory account of how the mother-wife may neutralize this conflict—she has no real threat as her daughter has already been castrated. We repeat the alternative explanation we have suggested. The mother counters the daughter's threat of abandonment by activating her shame of menstruation. This lowers her daughter's sense of self-esteem and leaves her daughter afraid to abandon her, leaving them in a mutual enmeshed relationship with each other. The wife-husband relationship, however, remains unchanged; the wife still envies her husband and the husband

13. Freud, "Consequences"; *Three Essays*.
14. Stephens, *Oedipus Complex*.

still deprecates his wife. The father will threaten to abandon his daughter while she still idealizes him. This leaves the daughter enmeshed with both father and mother.

As the superego is introjected in this process the daughter's moral identification with her mother has an enmeshed and symbiotic quality. This lays the foundation for a low self-esteem and an envy of men. Furthermore, this pathology, without corrective therapy, is likely to reproduce itself from generation to generation. The enmeshed daughter will herself grow up to be an enmeshed mother. If she marries a disengaged man, this pattern will be repeated in the next generation.

Let us summarize these patterns.

1. The mother is afraid that her daughter will abandon her as she grows up.

2. The father acts quite indifferent to his daughter, forcing her to chase after him.

3. To keep from being abandoned, the mother attempts to diminish her daughter's self-esteem by evoking a shame of menstruation in her.

4. As a result, the daughter reaches an enmeshed relationship with her mother, giving up her overt attempts to abandon her mother. As the introjection of the Freudian superego occurs as a function of the resolution of the feminine Oedipus or Electra Complex, the daughter's morality is based on shame and displays an enmeshed quality.

The Biblical Narrative

The biblical book of Ruth is the paradigmatic mother-daughter relationship in the Hebrew Bible, though it actually describes the relationship between mother-in-law and daughter-in-law. It portrays a very different view of mother-daughter relationships than that emergent in Greek tragedies. Naomi moves with her prosperous husband and two sons from Bethlehem in Judah to Moab. There Naomi's husband dies, and the sons also die after marrying Moabite women—Orpah and Ruth. Bereft of both family and wealth, Naomi decides to return to Bethlehem. Orpah and Ruth insisted on accompanying her. As much as Naomi could have benefited from the support and companionship of two young women, she nevertheless unselfishly urges them to return to their families of origin in Moab. Orpah leaves but Ruth stays with Naomi who still seeks to persuade her to leave.[15] Ruth replies with one of the most beautiful of all speeches in Scripture.

> Entreat me not to leave thee, or to return from following after thee: for whither thou goest, I will go; and where thou lodgest, I will lodge: thy people shall be my people, and thy God my God . . . [16]

Ruth's good character and her kindness to Naomi become known in Bethlehem and attract the notice of Boaz, a wealthy and dignified community leader, and a kinsman of Naomi's husband. Naomi helped facilitate a match between Ruth and Boaz to give Ruth "a resting place which will be good for you."[17] Ruth remains devoted to her former mother-in-law who acted so unselfishly toward her.

Boaz marries Ruth, and in due course, a baby son, Obed, is born . . . Naomi becomes the nurse, taking the infant into her arms. The women of Bethlehem affirm her joy saying, "A son is born to Naomi."[18] By giving her daughter-in-law her blessing to grow, Naomi becomes reintegrated into her daughter's new family. The baby Obed becomes the grandfather of King David.

The covenantal matrix within which a daughter develops is symbolized by the ritual purification (*Laws of Niddah*) in relation to her.[19] Though not mentioned in the story of Ruth, this act fundamentally changes all familial relationships. Menstruation need not cause the same diminution in self-esteem as in many pagan societies. Biblical civilization transforms this bodily process into part of the woman's unique gift. In practice, the essential *Laws of Niddah* is that a woman avoids sexual contact with her husband from the onset of her menstrual period. Seven days after the termination of her menstrual flow, she may cleanse herself in the ritual water of the *mikvah*, after which full sexual contact between husband and wife may be resumed.[20] Importantly, only women are involved in this ritual ceremony. A woman's sexuality is accepted as normal, and not as a cause for shame, and is not dependent on male attitudes.

15. Ruth 1:15.
16. Ruth 1:16–17.
17. Ruth 3:1.
18. Ruth 4:14–15.
19. Lev 15:19–28.
20. Blumenkrantz, *Laws of Niddah*; Tendler, *Pardes Rimonim*.

The father's transformation in the family is pivotal. He is transformed from child exposer/abandoner to protector, resolving the daughter's Electra Complex and strengthening her hold on life. Parents can relate in a truly nurturing manner to their daughters and to each other, and they provide genuine protection and support the daughter's need for healthy development. Leaving her parents' house to become a mother on her own is a joyous and sacred fulfillment of her duty as a woman of valor.[21]

The biblical family, once again, is purposive. The biblical husband honors and respects his wife. His wife in turn, helps him to pass on the covenant and guide her daughter in her development as a woman. Essential to this is both mother and daughter accepting their femininity and womanness without shame. The daughter gives up any attempt to abandon her mother and ally with her father, instead growing at her own pace through acceptance of nurturance from her mother and protection from her father without being symbiotically connected to either. She is able to love without becoming enmeshed and can go into a mature relationship as a full personality.

Let us summarize the biblical pattern as follows.

1. The mother encourages her daughter to leave her own life and is not afraid of being abandoned by her.

2. The father is protective towards his daughter in her development

3. To enhance her daughter's development and self-esteem as a woman, the mother participates in the *mikvah* ceremony which normalizes and even celebrates her daughter's menstrual cycle.

4. The daughter arrives at a non-enmeshed healthy relationship with her mother. As the introjection of the biblical superego for the daughter can be said to occur as a function of the resolution of the Ruth narrative, the daughter's morality is based on a solid and independent sense of self (i.e., the Ruth Motif).

A Contemporary Illustration

The tragic implications of the Greek mother-daughter relationship are illustrated graphically in Alfonso Arau's 1992 Mexican film, *Like Water*

---

21. *b. Genesis Rabbah* 26:4.

for Chocolate.[22] This film is adapted from a novel by the same name and portrays a love story that takes place in Mexico in the era of the Mexican Revolution. The main characters are Tita de la Garza, the protagonist, and Pedro, her love interest. Pedro and his father come to ask for Tita's hand in marriage. Tita's mother, Mama Elena, refuses. The de la Garza family tradition demands the youngest daughter must remain unmarried and take care of her mother until death. However, Mama Elena offers Rosaura's hand instead, and Pedro accepts in order to be closer to Tita.

Mama Elena keeps a close watch on Tita and Pedro. When Tita finds an excuse not to attend Rosaura's engagement party, Mama Elena forces Tita to prepare the wedding banquet as punishment. Tita's desire for Pedro is put into her cooking, and as a result, the wedding guests are overcome by "intoxication" and a longing for their true love. The wedding ends with all the guests crying and vomiting by the river. Even Mama Elena unlocks a box and holds a photograph of a man who is thought to be her true love.

One night one year later, Pedro goes to Tita. When Tita awakens to use the restroom, Pedro waits in the shadows nearby for her return. He kisses her passionately. Suddenly, Mama Elena wakes up, looking and calling for Tita. Mama Elena asks Tita where she has been, does not believe Tita's answer, and the next day Mama Elena sends Rosaura, Pedro, and their baby boy to Texas. Soon, they receive news that the baby died on the way to Texas. In an act of rebellion, Tita blames her mother; Mama Elena responds by smacking Tita across the face with a wooden spoon, which breaks her nose. Tita secludes herself after the incident. Mama Elena states there is no place for "lunatics" on the farm and wants her to be institutionalized. However, Dr. John Brown (who had been summoned for the birth of Rosaura's now deceased child) decides to take care of Tita at his home instead. While caring for Tita, Dr. Brown tells Tita a story from his Native American grandmother. The story says that all humans are born with enough matches to burn like a candle. But to set off this fire, every person must find their own trigger. They must also be careful to not set off all their internal matches at once, or risk immolation. Tita eventually enters into a relationship with Dr. Brown, even planning to marry him at one point, but she cannot shake her feelings for Pedro.

22. Arau, *Like Water for Chocolate.*

Mama Elena is seriously wounded when rebels attack the ranch. Tita rushes to her mother's side. Soon after, Mama Elena dies. Rosaura and Pedro return for the funeral, which causes sexual tension between Tita and Pedro. Rosaura soon gives birth to a second child, a girl, and is told that due to complications she will never be able to have another child. Rosaura declares that her daughter, Esperanza, will never marry because she will have to take care of her mother, repeating the pathology that occurred between her mother Elena and her younger sister Tita.

Dr. Brown is called away and after dinner one night, Pedro once again confronts Tita. He takes her to a bed and makes love to her. Though Rosaura and her sister Chencha see "phosphorescent plumes" and a strange glow coming from the room, they refuse to go near, fearing that the commotion is the ghost of Mama Elena. After that night, Tita fears that she is pregnant.

Rosaura feels that Tita isn't a threat to her marriage and asks for her help to win back Pedro's affection. Rosaura asks if Tita would place her on a special diet so that she could lose weight and cure bad breath. Rosaura leaves the kitchen and Mama Elena's ghost enters. She scolds Tita for her relationship with Pedro and curses the baby growing in Tita's stomach. Another character Gertrudis tells Tita that she needs to accept her relationship with Pedro and get an abortion by bathing in vinegar.

Mama Elena's ghost returns and asks Tita to leave the ranch. Tita stands up to her mother and declares her autonomy. As a result, the ghost shrinks into a tiny light. The fiery light of Mama Elena's ghost falls on Pedro, setting him on fire. Tita rescues him, cares for him, and helps him in recovering.

While Tita nurses Pedro back to health, Dr. Brown returns. After his return, Tita tells Dr. Brown that she cannot marry him because she gave her virginity to another. Dr. Brown vows that it does not matter to him because he loves her and still wants to marry her, but says he will respect her wishes.

Twenty years pass. The audience learns each person's fate through conversations at the wedding of Rosaura's daughter Esperanza to the son of Dr. Brown. Rosaura suspiciously died of a gastronomical disease three days after an argument between Rosaura and Tita about Esperanza's future. At the wedding reception, Pedro confesses to Tita that he still loves her, wants to marry her, and has dreamed of their wedding day.

The movie ends with Tita and Pedro making love in a candle-lit barn. As Dr. Brown had warned years before, Tita and Pedro's passions ignite too quickly, and Pedro dies just as he has a sensuous orgasm. Tita swallows matches to self-immolate, lighting the entire ranch on fire in the process. Esperanza returns to the ranch and finds only Tita's cookbook, which contains her recipes and tells of her and Pedro's love story.

In the final scene, Esperanza's daughter, also named Tita, ends by saying, "My Mother, how I miss her cooking. The smell of her kitchen. Her talking while she prepared the meals. Her Christmas rolls. Mine never come out like hers. For some reason I can't make myself stop crying when I make them. It must be that I am as sensitive to onions as Tita, my great aunt. She'll continue to live as long as someone continues to cook her recipes."

This movie illustrates vividly the potentially pathological effects of a mother trying to enmesh her daughter because she is afraid of being abandoned. How different this narrative is from that of Ruth where Naomi gladly helps Ruth find a husband and indeed becomes the nurse for their son, Obed.

≈ ≈ ≈

PSYCHO-BIBLICAL GUIDE SIX

Nurture your daughter and do not keep her from living her own life. Naomi does not try to enmesh her daughter-in-law Ruth after Ruth's husband dies, but facilitates Ruth's marriage to Boaz. Ruth returns the favor and brings Naomi back into the family as a "grandmother." Electra, in contrast, hates her mother Clytemnestra for not supporting her and for murdering her husband and Electra's father, Agamemnon. Electra responds by murdering her mother. Learn how to support your daughter and encourage her to succeed to the utmost of her abilities. Do not be afraid she will abandon you, but encourage her to develop her own life if she can.

7

Relating to Siblings

**PSYCHO-BIBLICAL ISSUE SEVEN
(PRIMARILY TO A PARENT RELATING TO SONS):**

*I feel differently about each of my children and think they are different
from one another. Do I treat them the same way on principle or follow
my feelings and my perceptions?*

BOTH THE HEBREW BIBLE and the literature of ancient Greece present
stories of family conflict. However, several basic differences between
these literatures can be quickly noted. The stories of Genesis abound with
sibling conflict, portraying sons vying for paternal approval and blessing. The earliest myths of ancient Greece are very different, portraying
conflict between father and son rather than between brothers, with the
brothers often banding together, joined by the mother to kill or castrate
the menacing father.[1]

The second basic difference between the literatures is even more
striking. The Hebrew Bible offers a plan to resolve family conflict by em-
ploying the father's blessing. Originally the source of the sibling conflict,
the father's blessing may work to achieve some level of reconciliation between his sons, as in Jacob's tailored blessings to each of his sons (actually

1. See the psycho-historical reconstruction of primitive man by Freud, *Totem and
Taboo.*

ten of his twelve sons, and two of his grandsons). Greek literature offers no such balm, never developing the idea that a father should bless his children. The result is that conflict in the families grows more angry and nasty in each succeeding generation until the families self-destruct, as did the family of Oedipus.

Greek Narratives

The Greek family is essentially purposeless. The father is not a source of inheritance but an impediment. The Greek myths, in contrast, never develop the idea that a father should bless his children or pass anything down to him. Instead he actually rejects them. Sibling rivalry is initially masked by the threat of the father to the sons who must band together to protect themselves. However, this bonding is shallow and will disappear as the paternal threat recedes. The result is that conflict in the families grows more angry and nasty in each succeeding generation, until the families self-destruct. Let us examine four Greek narratives in this regard, arranged chronologically: 1) Ouranos and Cronus, 2) Cronus and Zeus, 3) Zeus and Heracles, and 4) Oedipus and his sons.

1. Ouranos and His Sons

Sky (Ouranos) is portrayed as a menacing figure, hating his sons from the first. As soon as each is born, Ouranos shoves him back into Earth (Gaia) for fear of being usurped. He is described as "enjoying his wickedness." Groaning in pain, Gaia bands her sons together and urges them to take vengeance against their father; she gives Cronus a saw-toothed scimitar. Cronus cuts off his father's genitals while he is lying down, stretched out fully against Gaia, longing for love. Ouranos reproaches his sons and calls them Titans, for he says, "They strained in insolence and did a deed for which they would be punished afterwards."[2]

The sons do have a common purpose, but it is based on fear of the father rather than in any anticipation of a blessing. This mirrors the Greeks' relationship to their gods. Indeed, Ouranos warned his sons that they

2. Hesiod, *Theogony,* lines 155–210. In Aollodorus's (1:1–3) version of this narrative cited in chapter 3, Ouranos throws his sons into Tartarus, in Hades, rather than shoving them back into Gaia. The events than proceed similarly in the two accounts.

would be punished for their misdeeds. The banding together of the sons is defensive against a hated father who threatens to destroy them. They accomplish identification through incorporation, and the father's curse is lurking in the background, threatening to punish them. Indeed, after the threat of Ouranos recedes, the previously repressed sibling rivalry has a chance to emerge: Cronus himself, according to some interpretations, imprisons his brothers, the Titans.[3]

2. Cronus and His Sons

This same pattern of a paternal threat to the sons emerges in the next generation as well. Cronus begets many children by force, and he proceeds to swallow them because he has learned from Gaia and Ouranos that his destiny is to be overcome by one of his sons. Rhea, Cronus' sister and wife, appeals to their parents, who send her to bear her youngest son, Zeus, in Crete. Rhea tricks Cronus into swallowing a huge stone in swaddling clothes by making him think he is swallowing Zeus. When Zeus grows up, he leads his siblings, the Olympian gods, to overthrow his father Cronus and his allies, the Titans. They hurl Cronus and their uncles down to Tartarus.[4] Yet, Zeus and his siblings do not need to cooperate after that in any meaningful way. Once again, we have a case where the sons (Zeus and the other Olympian gods) band together not out of any positive sense of purpose but as a defensive necessity against their threatening father, Cronus.

3. Zeus, Heracles, and Iphicles

Our third example of the relationship between paternal threat and sibling rivalry can be seen in Ovid's narrative of Heracles and Iphicles. Although the two boys are described as twins born of the same mother, Alcmene, they have different fathers. Heracles is the son of Zeus, while Iphicles, his twin, is the son of Alcmene's husband, Amphitryon. This has occurred as a result of Zeus's impersonation of Amphitryon during the latter's absence. Despite this trickery, neither father seems to be a threat in the sense that Ouranos and Cronus are. However, they seem largely absent or

3. Hesiod, *Theogony*, lines 504–5.
4. Ibid., 629–725.

powerless. Zeus boasts that he has fathered a son, whom he provocatively names Heracles (which means ironically "the glory of Hera"), who will rule the noble house of Perseus. However, Zeus is tricked by his enraged, betrayed wife Hera, who delays Heracles' birth long enough so that Zeus's promise goes instead to a relative, Eurystheus, who is born just before. [5]

4. Oedipus and His Sons

The final Greek family we examine is that of Oedipus himself—that is, his relationship to his sons rather than to his father. Two sons, Eteocles and Polyneices (as well as two daughters, Antigone and Ismene), were born of the incestuous union of Oedipus and Jocasta. After the suicide of Jocasta and the self-blinding of Oedipus, Polyneices and Eteocles, who were to share the power in Thebes, mistreat their now powerless father. They allow him to be exiled from Thebes, and he wanders about, cared for by his daughters. But before his death, Oedipus announces a curse on his sons: they shall die each at the hand of the other. According to the legend, Eteocles, now declared king of Thebes, exiles his brother. Polyneices, in turn, leads a vast army from Argos against Thebes in order to seize the throne for himself. In the ensuing battle, the brothers slay each other in individual combat, fulfilling their father's curse. This episode is so striking that it has been covered from slightly different angles by a number of Greek plays. In Sophocles' *Oedipus at Colonus*, Oedipus disowns his two sons and curses them to kill each other. He says to one son, Polyneices:

> And thou, begone, abhorred of me and unfathered!—begone, thou vilest of the vile, and with thee take my curse which I call down on thee never to vanquish the land of thy race . . . but by a kindred hand to die, and slay him by whom thou hast been driven out. I call the Destroying God who hath set that dreadful hatred in you twain. Go with these words in thine ears . . . that Oedipus has divided such honours to his sons.[6]

Oedipus's conduct is diametrically opposite to the blessing of Jacob discussed below, even Jacob's mixed blessing on Simeon and Levi! Jacob criticizes Simeon and Levi for their violent ways, but he does not disown

---

5. Hesiod, *Shield of Heracles*, lines 35, 56 and 80.

6. Sophocles, *Oedipus at Colonus*, lines 1386–94.

them. Oedipus disowns Polyneices and Eteocles and curses them to be violent against each other.

Aeschylus, in *The Seven against Thebes*, describes the curse of Oedipus as follows:

> And both alike, even now and here have closed their suit, with steel for arbiter. And lo, the fury-fiend of Oedipus, their sire, hath brought his curse to consummation dire. Each in the left side smitten, see them laid— the children of one womb, slain by a mutual doom![7]

Again, note the striking difference between this curse and the prophecy given by God of the Scriptures to the pregnant Rebecca regarding Jacob and Esau.[8] Polyneices and Eteocles are cursed to a mutuality of doom, within one womb; Jacob and Esau are described as two separate nations, albeit of the same womb. In both Sophocles and Aeschylus, Jocasta is described as already dead. Euripides' *The Phoenissae* presents a revised version: here Oedipus and Jocasta are still alive, and Jocasta engages in a futile attempt to bring about reconciliation between the two brothers. She describes Oedipus's curse as the product of his mental illness:

> He [Oedipus] is still living in the palace, but his misfortunes have so unhinged him that he imprecates the most unholy curse on his sons, praying that they may have to draw the sword before they share the house between them.[9]

Unlike Rebecca, Jocasta fails to bring about a peaceful reconciliation between her sons, indicating that, even when the Greek mother tries to resolve sibling rivalry, she is unsuccessful.

In summary, the Greek family is purposeless. The father is not a source of inheritance but an impediment. Sibling rivalry is initially masked by the threat of the father to the sons who must band together to protect themselves. However, this bonding is shallow and will disappear as the paternal threat recedes. This pattern is consummated in the curse of Oedipus to his two sons to slay each other. The decline of the father allows the emergence of the previously latent sibling rivalry, which

7. Aeschylus, *Seven Against Thebes,* lines 879–924.

8. Gen 25:23–24.

9. Euripides, *Phoenissae,* lines 1–91.

culminates in the mutual killing of Oedipus's two sons, Polyneices and Eteocles, at the seventh gate of Thebes.

The following four issues are central to sibling relations in Greek narratives.

1. The father sees his sons as a threat to displace or kill him. He has no blessings to give them or a covenant to pass down. Rather, the ancient Greek father is trying to destroy or block his sons.

2. The sons band together to fight off the assaults of their father. They are not fighting with each other to inherit from him, but simply want to keep their father from destroying them.

3. This lack of sibling rivalry is misleading, not indicating any great love between brothers, but simply representing a necessary mutual survival pact.

4. As the father's power recedes (e.g., when Oedipus blinds himself), he curses his sons to kill each other—which they do!

Biblical Narratives

The biblical command to love and fear God denotes more of a sense of awe and respect rather than a fear of a capricious and vengeful deity. Therefore blessings from God and from one's father are important. Interestingly, the Hebrew Scriptures do not mention fathers blessing sons before Abraham. However, the blessing became increasingly important with each generation of the patriarchs, until Jacob becomes able, with his blessing, both to affirm the unity of his twelve sons as the basis of the twelve tribes of Israel and to recognize and encourage the unique individual qualities of each, and thus dampen sibling rivalry. We focus on four generations of biblical families: (1) Adam and his sons, (2) Abraham and his sons, (3) Isaac and his sons, and (4) Jacob and his sons. Across these four generations, fathers offer greater degrees of blessing, indeed differentiated blessing, and ultimately the resolution of sibling rivalry.

1. Adam and His Sons

The Hebrew Bible portrays God alone as giving blessings to all mankind at creation: "Then God blessed them, and God said to them, 'Be fruitful and multiply; fill the earth and subdue it; have dominion over the fish of the sea, over the birds of the air, and over every living thing that moves on the earth.'"[10] God also gave blessings directly to Adam and Eve and to Noah and his family.[11] But there is no indication that God blessed Cain and Abel directly or that Adam gave either son a blessing.

Consider the Genesis account. Cain, the elder, is a tiller of the ground, while Abel, the younger, is a keeper of sheep. Each brings an offering to the Lord, who has respect for Abel's offering, but not for Cain's. According to the traditional interpretation, God rejects Cain's offering because of the poor spirit in which Cain offers it. Although God accepts Abel's offering and does not accept Cain's, there is no indication in the text that God would not have accepted the sacrifices of both Cain and Abel, had they both been given in full spirit. Nevertheless, God specifically addresses Cain's disappointment and tries to address and defuse any jealousy Cain may feel towards Abel.

We have discussed this issue at length in chapter 2 but it is worth repeating here. First, God acknowledges Cain's disappointment: "Why are you angry? And why has your countenance fallen?"[12] Then he offers Cain the potential for acceptance if he changes: "If you do well, will you not be accepted?" Finally, God warns Cain of the dangers of a continuing bad spirit: "And if you do not do well, sin lies at the door. And its desire is for you, but you should rule over it."[13]

Nevertheless, God's intervention fails, and Cain murders Abel. Cain interprets his rejection in a classical Greek rather than a biblical way. He is in a zero-sum contest with Abel. In his mind he has been rejected because God preferred Abel, and out of anger and jealousy, he slays him. When God subsequently asks Cain, "Where is Abel thy brother?" Cain responds "I know not; am I my brother's keeper?" Cain could have answered simply, "I know not." But his adding "am I my brother's keeper?" reveals his obsession with Abel. Cain is in fact blaming Abel for Cain's own failing, rather than trying to improve on it himself.[14]

10. Gen 1:28.

11. Gen 1:28; 9:1.

12. Gen 4:6.

13. Gen 4:7.

14. Yoram Hazony (2012) provocatively argues that it is actually Cain, the farmer, who is obedient to God's command that man, after his expulsion from Eden, work the ground from which he was taken. (Gen 3.17–19, 23) Hazony, *Philosophy of Hebrew*, Ch. 4.

Notably absent in this account is any mention of direct communication between Adam or Eve and the two sons. Could Adam and Eve have been that unaware of the rivalry developing between Cain and Abel, and of Cain's jealousy toward Abel? Adam's direct blessing of his sons, showing each his place in the larger divine purpose, may have helped prevent the murder.

2. Abraham and His Sons

God tells Abraham that he himself will be a living blessing and that through him all the peoples of the world will be blessed. The ability to bless people is given over to Abraham and passed on to his descendants.[15] It seems clear that Abraham has developed a strong affection for Ishmael, his son by the Egyptian woman Hagar. Indeed, he entreats God on Ishmael's behalf when he is told that Sarah would bear him a child. "And Abraham said to God, 'Oh that Ishmael might live before You!'"[16]

Significantly, God responds to Abraham's entreaty by informing him that he has blessed Ishmael but will establish his covenant only with Isaac.

> "And as for Ishmael, I have heard you. Behold, I have blessed him, and will make him fruitful, and will multiply him exceedingly and I will make him a great nation. But my covenant I will establish with Isaac, whom Sarah shall bear to you at this set time next year."[17]

Abraham circumcises both Ishmael and Isaac. According to some interpretations (Rabbi Nehemiah), Abraham gives his blessing only to Isaac, though others (Rabbi Hama) interpret Abraham as giving only gifts to Isaac.[18] What is clear is that Abraham sends Ishmael out into the desert because he scoffed at a feast celebrating the weaning of Isaac. Subsequently, Abraham trains Isaac as his successor and the receiver of God's special covenant. He gives his other sons gifts and sends them away eastward.

Meanwhile, Abraham has apparently become close to Ishmael after a period of estrangement, and Ishmael and Isaac join together to bury

15. *b. Genesis Rabbah* 39:11; *Tanhuma Buber Lekh Lekha* 5; *Numbers Rabbah* 11:2; *Sota* 14.

16. Gen 17:18.

17. Gen 17:20–21.

18. *b. Genesis Rabbah* 61:6; Rashi on Gen 25:9, *Midrash Rabba*.

Abraham. Nevertheless, there is no indication of any real meeting of minds between the two sons. Isaac and Ishmael do seem to be able to cooperate when necessary, and one does not kill the other. However, they seem to pursue largely separate paths without any real common purpose, though Isaac's son Esau does later marry the daughter of Ishmael.[19]

3. Isaac and His Sons

Esau, the son of Isaac and Rebecca, has angrily threatened to kill Jacob, his twin brother. He accuses Jacob of stealing his birthright and his father's blessing. However, years later the brothers are reconciled and they coexist at least in peace if not in harmony of purpose. These peaceful outcomes of potentially explosive sibling clashes can result only because the parents, Isaac and Rebecca, do not saddle their sons with insurmountable emotional burdens; instead, they try to be supportive of their sons. God first tells Rebecca, when she is still pregnant with Jacob and Esau, that there are two great nations in her womb and that the older will serve the younger.[20] This is more a prediction than a blessing per se. God subsequently does bless Jacob but does not seem specifically to bless Esau. Again, note the similarity here to the biblical theme of birth order that is discussed in the Jacob and Esau story—but with a very different purpose. Hera acts out of personal pique; Rebecca—and even Sarah—act out of a sense of suitability of inheritance.

Isaac, however, does bless both Jacob and Esau, repeating God's prediction that the older (Esau) shall serve the younger (Jacob). Significantly, however, he gives each son a blessing that seemed suitable for each one. First Isaac blesses Jacob, who has disguised himself as Esau, with the dew of the heaven and the leadership of other nations. Esau, distraught over Jacob's trickery, also receives a blessing of the dew of the heaven, but is destined to live by the sword and to serve his brother. Esau naturally hates Jacob because he believes that the latter has stolen his blessing from him, and so he threatens to kill him.[21] But their mother Rebecca's intervention restores peace between the brothers, and ultimately Esau indicates

19. Gen 28:9.
20. Gen 25:23–24.
21. Gen 27:39–41.

satisfaction with his portion: "I have plenty, my brother."[22] The fact that Esau has also been blessed by his father gives him the resilience to gain great success. Significantly, both of the twins find successful families and lines of kings. Again note that Rebecca succeeds in bringing about family harmony where Jocasta, the mother-wife of Oedipus, fails.

4. Jacob and His Sons

In the succeeding generations each father blesses his own children, joining them closer to the covenant with God and helping each son define and affirm his own sense of identity. The father permits and encourages them to enjoy the good things of life, both spiritual and material. Jacob, however, has the joy of seeing his sons reconciled despite their many problems with both him and each other. Even the selling of Joseph into slavery in Egypt ends positively when Joseph, as viceroy of Egypt, saves his family from famine in such a psychologically wise way that the old wounds are appreciably healed and the trauma emerging from them dissipates.[23]

The biblical narrative does not specify a direct blessing that God gives to Jacob's sons. But Jacob, in his last moments, conscientiously and lovingly blesses his sons, each according to his own personality and his own needs. Going a step further, he also blesses his grandsons Ephraim and Manasseh (Joseph's sons) and adds that they would be the highest examples of blessing: "By you Israel will bless, saying, 'May God make you as Ephraim and as Manasseh.'"[24] It is important to note that Jacob uses the blessing to prepare each son for the unique problems and challenges of his own personal situation. This recognition of the unique history and characteristic of each son does much to deflate the potential dangers of sibling rivalries and of parent-child conflicts.

For example, when Jacob blesses his sons, he criticizes Simeon and Levi for their violent ways: "Simeon and Levi are brothers; instruments of cruelty are in their dwelling place."[25] Brotherhood must have a positive purpose and consist of more than simply being violent together. Still, Jacob does not disown Simeon and Levi, or curse them, as does Oedipus his

22. Gen 33:4.
23. Gen 37–45.
24. Gen 48:20.
25. Gen 49:5.

sons in the narrative presented previously. Instead, Jacob scatters Simeon and Levi in Israel rather than giving them their own territory.

These four biblical generations show an increase in paternal involvement, a greater degree of paternal blessing, and ultimately a differentiated blessing to each son. This differentiated blessing seems crucial in diminishing sibling rivalry.[26]

The following four issues are central to sibling relations in biblical narratives.

1. The father sees his sons as a blessing. He does not try to block them but sees them as his inheritance in passing down the covenant he has with God.

2. The sons compete with each other to be their father's favorite. Each wants his father's blessing and to be chosen to carry on the biblical covenant.

3. This sibling rivalry is initially murderous (Cain killing Abel). However, it becomes dampened a bit in each succeeding generation as the father blesses his children more fully and the mother intervenes as a peace-maker.

4. Jacob initially plays favorites, preferring Joseph to his brothers and later Benjamin, both sons of his favorite wife Rachel. However before his death, Jacob differentiates his blessing across all his sons (and two grandsons), each according to his abilities and temperament. Thus, each of the twelve sons of Israel (Jacob) receives a blessing designed uniquely for him. This greatly dampens sibling rivalry.

---

26. The lack of a differentiated blessing seems to be a critical issue in the ferocious conflict between some of King David's sons, all born of different mothers. "And sons are born David in Hebron. And his firstborn was Amnon by Ahinoam the Jezreelite . . . And the third was Absalom son of Maacah daughter of Talmai king of Geshur. And the fourth was Adonijah, son of Haggith . . . " (2 Sam 3:2–5). Absalom, for example, orders his henchmen to slay his half-brother Amnon in retaliation for the latter's raping of Absalom's full-sister Tamar (2 Sam 1). This in itself seems to have nothing to do with conflict over inheriting David's kingship. Later, however, Solomon is born to David and Bathsheba (2 Sam 5:13–16), and more to the point, Adonijah does attempt to displace Solomon and succeed David to the Kingship of Israel. With the help of his mother, Bathsheba, Solomon ultimately succeeds in becoming king and has his half-brother Adonijah killed (1 Kgs 1–2). What makes this narrative different from that of Joseph and his brothers is that there is only one kingship, and in this sense, the inheritance and blessing cannot be differentiated and thus shared.

A Contemporary Illustration

Legends of the Fall is a 1994 epic film drama directed by Edward Zwick and based on the 1979 novella of the same title by Jim Harrison.[27] It stars Brad Pitt, Anthony Hopkins, and Aidan Quinn. The film's timeframe spans the decade in America before World War I through the Prohibition era, and into the 1930s, ending with a brief scene set in 1963. The film centers on the Ludlow family of Montana, including a veteran of the Indian Wars, Colonel Ludlow, and his sons, Alfred, Tristan, and Samuel, and object of the brothers' love, Susannah.

Sick of the betrayals the United States government has perpetrated on Native Americans, Colonel William Ludlow retires to a remote part of Montana with One Stab, a Native American friend, where they build a ranch. The Colonel's wife, Isabel, does not adapt to the harsh winters of Montana and moves to the East Coast. Colonel Ludlow thus raises his three sons alone, all dramatically different from one another. Throughout the film, we watch the brothers grow and develop very different characters. Alfred is responsible and cautious and is driven and determined to make a life away from the mountains in the "big city." He is the somber, sober, and conscientious older brother. He wants desperately to gain his father's approval as he feels his father has always been biased towards Tristan. Tristan, the middle brother, is wild and well-versed in American Indian traditions, happier at home, working and living from the land. He is a bit irresponsible but seems to draw people's affection naturally. Samuel, the youngest, is educated but naive and constantly watched over by his brothers. Yet in some ways he is more thoughtful than his older brothers.

Though different, the three brothers mature and seem to have an unbreakable bond—that is, until Susanna enters their lives. When Samuel, the youngest of the three, returns from college he brings with him his beautiful fiancée, Susanna. The eldest son, Alfred, soon finds himself in love with his brother's fiancée, and things get worse when he discovers a growing passion between Susanna and Tristan. As the brothers set out to fight a war in Europe, suspicion and jealousy threaten to tear apart their once indestructible bond.

The question we pose is how Colonel Ludlow fathers his three sons, and whether he does this in a Greek or biblical way. The brothers, though

27. Zwick, *Legends of the Fall*.

close, do not band together against their father as in the Greek narratives. Instead, they follow the biblical narratives in each wanting to be loved by their father. Ludlow loves Samuel as his youngest, and genuinely mourns him when he is killed in the War. And he has come to depend very much on Alfred and his practical, conscientious manner. Nevertheless, Tristan seems to draw his father's love effortlessly, perhaps because Tristan reminds him of himself. And Alfred expresses his resentment that his father has always preferred Tristan.

This seems to parallel the feelings of the brothers of Joseph resenting the fact that he is his father Jacob's favorite. The end of the story of Jacob provides a brilliant resolution to his relationship with all of his sons. He gives each of them (actually ten sons and two grandsons) a unique blessing and inheritance. Colonel Ludlow does not manage to do this.

~ ~ ~

PSYCHO-BIBLICAL GUIDE SEVEN

Do not be afraid to treat different children differently. You must love each of them uniquely as they are different from one another. You make a mistake by trying to treat all of them the same way. What is important is that you bless each of them in a way that recognizes each's unique personhood. Individualize your blessing to each child as did Jacob and do not foster competition between them. By all means, do not act like Oedipus and curse your children to hurt each other.

8

Relating Body to Soul

PSYCHO-BIBLICAL ISSUE EIGHT:

How should I integrate my body and my soul? If I spend too much time on my physical appearance does this make me shallow? If I spend all my time in spiritual pursuits, does this make me unattractive? Do I need to separate my soul from my body, and vice-versa, or can they work together?

THE BIBLICAL AND GREEK worlds present dramatically different views of the relationship between body and soul. In Plato's thinking, the relationship between body and soul is conflictual and unfortunate. "The soul is a helpless prisoner chained hand and foot in the body, compelled to view reality not directly but only through its prison bars, and wallowing in their ignorance."[1] The body itself is seen as entrapping the soul and the highest form of control over one's self is the freedom to decide whether to continue to live or to die.

The biblical view is very different. It does not see the body as entrapping the soul but as supporting it in their joint service of God. Birth and death are events beyond human understanding that God alone will handle. The individual is given freedom in terms of following God's commandments.

1. Plato, *Phaedo*, 839.

The Greek Narrative

The earliest mention of the soul in Greek literature is Homer's morbid picture of the unhappy shadowy existence of the Trojan War heroes in Hades. Later Greek literature accepts the existence of souls but, in Platonic thought, tends to view the soul as very lofty and sacred and the body as being the soul's gross earthly prison. Homeric souls disappear like smoke, in the manner of ghosts, if someone attempts to touch them. They dwell in Hades and can only regain their vitality and memory by drinking blood.[2]

The Homeric notion of the soul remained current until Plato's times when an important change occurred. The soul was then "elevated" from a materialistically conceived double to a dematerialized divine being, of a nature totally different from the body (*soma*). Plato tells us that the Orphics (the followers of Orpheus) called the body a prison of the soul and that others with comparable ideas called it a tomb.[3]

Plato sees the relationship between body (*soma*) and soul (*psyche*) as conflictual and unfortunate. The soul (or *psyche*) is a helpless prisoner, chained hand and foot in the body, compelled to view reality not directly, but only through its prison bars, and wallowing in ignorance.[4] Again, in Plato's thinking, the relationship between body and soul is conflictual and unfortunate. He argues that the evil acts of the body pollute the soul and prevent it from achieving a complete and clean separation and returning to the world of ideal. Only the soul can perceive *ideal truth*, but it cannot do so as long as it must perceive reality by use of the five bodily senses. Thus, the real attainment of truth can come only in the higher world when souls can perceive directly without interference of the body. For, if pure knowledge is impossible while the body is with us, one of two things must follow: either it cannot be acquired at all or only when we are dead, for then the soul will be by itself apart from the body, but not before.[5]

The Platonic distrust of the body, especially the feminine body, is vividly expressed in the previously mentioned narrative of Ouranos and Gaia. Gaia, the earth goddess, colludes with her son Cronus to castrate

2. Homer, *Odyssey,* 11.25, 206.
3. *Oxford Dictionary,* 895.
4. Plato, *Phaedo,* 82d.
5. Ibid., 66e.

her husband Ouranos as he approaches her for sexual intercourse.[6] This distrust of the female body is continued in the portrayal of Pandora. She is described by Hesiod as a seductive but deceitful woman, sent by Zeus to be the "ruin of mankind." For Hesiod, "Zeus has made women to be an evil to mortal men, with a nature to do evil."[7] Indeed, one the few acceptable feminine figures in classical Greece was Athena, the virginal goddess of wisdom. Described as born from Zeus' head, she wears closely cropped hair and carries her aegis, topped by a Medusa head, away from her body. Thus, she has separated herself from dangerous female sexuality and becomes the personification of an abstract desexualized wisdom.

Plato portrays Socrates in his last days as viewing death as freeing the soul from the body in order to achieve pure knowledge and return to the world of *ideal forms*.[8] Indeed, for them, philosophy is "preparation for death"[9] and even "desire for death." Given the preference for death over life, it seems only a short step for Socrates to be asked, "Then why not suicide?" Socrates responds with his famous guard-post allegory as an argument against suicide. Life is a sorry business but we must not leave our guard-post unless we are relieved by the gods.[10] We will return specifically to this topic in chapter 9.

The Biblical Narrative

The Hebrew view is very different. There is none of the Platonic sense that the body must die to liberate the soul. Body and soul may or may not be different but need not be in conflict. Man must keep his body both physically and morally clean. Biblical thought views both the human body and soul as sacred (both referred to by the Hebrew noun *nefesh*), both created by God. They can and must function in harmony to fulfill God's purpose in the world. Though the body supports the soul in their joint service of God, there is none of the Platonic sense that the body must die to liberate the soul. Body and soul may or may not be different but need not be in conflict. Man must keep his body both physically and morally clean.[11]

6. Apollodorus, *Library*, 1.1.1.
7. Hesiod, *Works and Days*, lines 60–86; *Theogony*, lines 600–10.
8. Plato, *Phaedo*, 83a.
9. Ibid., 64a, 68a.
10. Ibid., 62b–c.
11. Buchler, *Types of Piety*.

The Rabbinic-Pharisaic position acknowledges that there is a conflict in the human psyche between the "good inclination" (*yetzer ha-tov*) and the "bad inclination" (*yetzer ha-rá*). However, both of these inclinations are understood as equally human, and neither of them is identified with the flesh or the body as opposed to the soul.[12] The great Pharisee Rabbi Hillel described the soul as a guest in the body; the body should keep itself fit in order to offer hospitality to so distinguished a guest. The body was neither an evil to be repressed nor a bastion of heroism to be glorified by Olympic victories. For Hillel, both physical and spiritual activities are part of man's fulfillment of his obligation to God. Just as a king appoints someone to keep his statue clean, man, created in the divine image, must keep his body clean.[13]

In Hebrew thought, the human body and soul are both sacred, both created by God. They can and must function in harmony to fulfill God's purposes in the world. Hebrew thought sees emotion, intellect, and body as all integral components of a human being with no opposition between body and soul or between flesh and spirit. Israeli scholar Ephraim Urbach argues that the Hebrew term *nefesh* must be understood as the whole of man rather than a disembodied *psyche* or *anima*.[14]

Consider the description of King David, perhaps the most human of all the biblical figures. Very spiritual, David is God-fearing, musically gifted, and poetic. However, David is also a man of the flesh. He can be intensely political, coarse at times, and certainly is not immune to sexual desires and appetite. David is not one-sided. He is a "man of the field," as is Esau, but is also a "quiet man," as is Jacob.[15] It is the blend between David's spiritual and physical that makes him so endlessly fascinating and so prototypical of the Jewish emphasis on the integration of body and soul

In the beginning of 1 Samuel 16, God instructs Samuel to find a replacement from among the sons of Jesse the Bethlehemite for Saul whom God has rejected and to anoint the son that God will choose to as the future King of Israel. The first seven sons are not what God has in mind, and

12. Maccoby, *Mythmaker*, 92–93. Maccoby argues that this is very different than Paul's metaphysical dualism between the law of the spirit (*pneuma*) and the law of the flesh (*sarx*). This dualism, maintains Maccoby, is a doctrine characteristic of Gnosticism rather than Hebrew or Pharisaic thinking. It may be seen as very Platonic as well.

13. *b. Avot of Rabbi Nathan* 2:33.

14. Urbach, *The Sages.*

15. Gen 25:27.

Samuel bids Jesse to call his youngest son. When the youngest son, David, arrives on the scene, he is described as "ruddy with fine eyes, and goodly to look on," suggesting a robust health and physical attractiveness." His ruddiness seems to make him closer in appearance to the physical Esau than to the more contemplative Jacob.[16] Yet God has previously instructed Samuel when he has rejected Eliab, Jesse's eldest son, not to be overly concerned with physical experience at the expense of underlying spirituality: "Look not to his appearance and to his lofty stature, for I have cast him aside. For not as man sees does God sees. For man sees with the eyes and the Lord sees with the heart."[17] David is clearly God's choice. "And the Lord said, 'Arise, anoint him for this is the one.'" From this day on, David is described as gripped with the spirit of the Lord.[18] From his first appearance, then, the interchange between David's physical and spiritual nature is emphasized.

This pattern continues as we proceed in this narrative. Saul becomes depressed as a result of God's abandonment of him and asks his servants to bring to him a man skilled in playing the lyre. The musical and poetic David is brought to him, and the way he is described can be seen as illustrating the integration of the physical (body) and the spiritual (soul). "Look, I have seen a son of Jesse the Bethlehemite, skilled in playing, a valiant fellow, a warrior, prudent in speech, a good-looking man, and the Lord is with him."[19]

In the next chapter, the spiritual, lyre-playing David volunteers to answer the challenge to battle issued by the giant Philistine warrior Goliath. Saul at first refuses David's request, responding that David is just a lad (whom he knows as his lyre-player). David persists, emphasizing his physical prowess, describing how he has already defeated a lion and a bear that threatened his father's flock. He says specifically to Saul, "The Lord who has rescued me from the lion and the bear will rescue me from the hand of this Philistine."[20]

Saul finally agrees and even clothes David in his own armor. Yet David rejects it as he not used to it and is clumsy in it. Instead David goes to face Goliath with a simple shepherd's pouch, in which he has put

16. Gen 25:19–33.
17. 1 Sam 16:6–7.
18. 1 Sam 16:13.
19. 1 Sam 16:18–19.
20. 1 Sam 17:8–11, 31–37.

five smooth stones and a slingshot. David, in other words, hopes to make up in agility what he lacks in brute strength. His strategy works and he strikes Goliath in the forehead with one stone from his slingshot and slays him. Yet central to this narrative is that David feels it is his spiritual relationship with the God of Israel, not his physical agility alone, which has led to Goliath's defeat. Before he runs at Goliath, David says to him: "And all this assembly shall know that not by sword and by spear does the Lord deliver, for the Lord's is the battle and he shall give you into our hand."[21]

Throughout his life, David displays this integration between the spiritual and the physical, playing the lyre and writing the most beautiful psalms and at the same time exhibiting a strong physical nature, being a skilled politician and a fierce warrior.

In later Talmudic thought, body and soul are differentiated somewhat, but with none of the flavor of complete disconnection so prevalent in Platonic writings. The contrasts between Greek and biblical views regarding the body-soul relationship are exemplified in the following passage, which contains a discussion between the Roman Emperor Antoninus (perhaps Marcus Aurelius) and Rabbi Judah the Prince, the man credited for composing the Mishna.[22]

> Antoninus said to the Rabbi: "The body and the soul can both free themselves from judgment. Thus, the body can plead: The soul has sinned, [the proof being] that from the day it left me I lie like a dumb stone in the grave [powerless to do aught]. Whilst the soul can say: The body has sinned, [the proof being] that from the day I departed from it I fly about in the air like a bird [and commit no sin]." He replied, "I will tell thee a parable. To what may this be compared? To a human king who owned a beautiful orchard which contained splendid figs. Now, he appointed two watchmen therein, one lame and the other blind. [One day] the lame man said to the blind, 'I see beautiful figs in the orchard. Come and take me upon thy shoulder, that we may procure and eat them.' So the lame bestrode the blind, procured and ate them. Sometime after, the owner of the orchard came and inquired of them, "Where are those beautiful figs?" The lame man replied, "Have I then feet to walk with?" The blind man replied, "Have I eyes to see with?" What did he do? He placed the lame upon the blind and judged

21. 1 Sam 17:38–54.

22. In the Jewish tradition, the Mishna or Oral Torah was given by God to Moses on Mt. Sinai in addition to the written Torah (Scriptures).

them together. So will the Holy One, blessed be He, bring the soul, [re]place it in the body, and judge them together, as it is written, *He shall call to the heavens from above, and to the earth, that he may judge his people. He shall call to the heavens from above*—this refers to the soul; *and to the earth, that he may judge his people*—this refers to the body.[23]

The integration of body and soul is nowhere more clearly expressed than in the opening words of Genesis 4. "And the man knew Eve his wife; and she conceived and bore Cain . . . "[24] Adam's spiritual and physical "knowing" of Eve are integrated. Even after the killing of Abel by Cain, this integration of spiritual and sexual knowledge is repeated. "And Adam knew his wife again, and she bore a son, and called his name Seth."[25]

The essential unity of spiritual and physical love runs throughout the Hebrew Bible and is nowhere more beautifully expressed than in Solomon's Song of Songs.

> Let him kiss me, with the kisses of his mouth—
> For thy love is better than wine . . .
> Tell me, O thou whom my soul loveth,
> Where thou feedest, where thou makest thy flock to rest at noon . . .
> Thy cheeks are comely with circlets,
> Thy neck with beads . . .
> Behold thou are fair my love; behold thou are fair;
> Thine eyes are as doves . . .
> By night on my bed I sought him whom my soul loveth;
> I sought him, but I found him not.
> I will rise now, and go about the city,
> In the streets and in the broad ways,
> I will seek him whom my soul loveth.
> I sought him, but I found him not . . .
> When I found him whom my soul loveth;
> I held him and would not let him go.[26]

23. *b. Sanhedrin* 91a–b.
24. Gen 4:1.
25. Gen 4:25.
26. Song 1–3.

Contemporary Illustrations

We present illustrations from two novels to illustrate our themes: the first, *Axel*, the nineteenth-century novel by the French romantic author Villiers de l'Isle-Adam,[27] and the second, the 1959 novella *The Transposed Heads*,[28] adapted by the great German novelist Thomas Mann from an Indian legend.

In the first illustration, Axel finally finds the woman for whom he has long been searching. As dawn approaches after a night of love, they envisage the life that lies before them; there is nothing they cannot see, nothing they cannot obtain. Their life and love stretch out in infinite perspective.

> "Come, let's leave at once," she cries; "throw on your coat. Outside the carriage horses are already pawing the morning dew. They'll take us past scented orange groves, and out on the roads people will soon be about. We shall pass villages and towns . . . Beyond, there will be more towns waking in the sunlight; the whole world will be waking. We can at last give reality to all our dreams."
>
> As she speaks dawn breaks. She lifts the curtain of the window.
>
> "Leave it alone," Axel says. "What do you want with the sun? Our dreams are too rare to be realized in the daylight."
>
> At first she does not understand him.
>
> "But look," she cries, "there is the world! Let's live!"
>
> "No," Axel answers. "Our existence is complete; our cup is now full. We've already exhausted the future. No clock can count the hours of this night—and what will the realities of tomorrow be worth compared to the visions what we've seen? . . .
>
> "Do you think such desires as ours will put up with the earth from day to day? Don't you see that the earth, this drop of congealed filth, has become the illusion? Don't you see that in our hearts we've done away with the love of life? It's in reality we've exchanged our souls. We owe it to ourselves not to accept this substitute—life . . . Let's leave the banquet, forever satisfied with this our moment. The poor fools, who can only measure reality by sensation, can have the pleasure of picking up the crumbs."[29]

The woman is at last persuaded by her lover's obsession with infinity and perfection and drinks the poison. "Since only the infinite tells the truth, we will go, forgetful of human speech, into our own infinity." Her

27. Villiers de l'Isle-Adam. *Axel.*

28. Mann, *Transposed Heads.*

29. Villiers de l'Isle-Adam. *Axel.*

own love of life integrating the spiritual and the physical is undone by Axel's Platonic elevation of the ideal over the real and being over becoming, and his Stoic idealization of suicide.

Let us now turn to the Mann novella The Transposed Heads. In the original Indian legend underlying this novel, two friends, one, Shridaman, wise but physically weak, and the other, Nanda, strong but mentally and spiritually weak, pursue the same woman. The woman is Sita, of luscious hips but mediocre intelligence. Sita chose the wise Shridaman to be her mate and all three went on a journey in which the men were attacked and beheaded. Sita magically brought both back to life, but mixed up the heads and bodies, and mistakenly put the wrong heads on the wrong bodies. This raised the question of who was the husband now? The answer was the man with the husband Shridaman's head, reflecting the supremacy of the head over the body.

In Mann's treatment, the dull-witted Nanda, now limited by Shridaman's weak physique becomes a hermit in the woods.. The intelligent and spiritual Shridaman, now endowed with Nanda's strong physique remains happily with Sita, but only for a time. Mann's treatment brings out sadder, funnier and more ironic twists than existed in the original legend, dealing with conflicts between head and body, and desire and fulfillment.

The trouble with both of these stories is that they represent an oppositional view of body and mind/soul and, analogously, the real and the ideal. In the first story, real life is portrayed as inferior to idealized infinity, and the Stoic and Platonic Axel convinces his biblically life-oriented lover to leave life with him. In the second story, the physically handsome figure is portrayed as an empty-head while the spiritual, intellectual figure is portrayed as physically unappealing. This inability to integrate a healthy body and soul is at the root of the Greek thinking we have presented in this chapter. There is absolutely no reason, from a biblical point of view, for the physically robust person not to be also spiritually and intellectually developed. The Hebrew conception of freedom does not involve freeing the soul from the body, but in developing a healthy integration between the two. The ideal infinite is also not superior to one's on-going real life.

∼ ∼ ∼

PSYCHO-BIBLICAL GUIDE EIGHT

Respect both body and soul. Do not concentrate on one at the expense of the other or as separate unrelated aspects of life. Spiritual wholeness will be reflected in physical appearance and physical health will provide the support for spiritual enhancement. Always strive for a healthy integration between your body and soul.

9

Relating to a Self-Destructive Person

PSYCHO-BIBLICAL ISSUE NINE:

What do I do if I encounter a person who is threatening to hurt or even kill himself? Do I respect his wishes or do I try to prevent him from hurting himself. Do I concentrate on preventing suicide or promoting life? In this context, how do I counter the sense of the heroic in suicide? How do I promote meaning in life? How do I apply this to myself?

THE BIBLICAL AND GREEK worlds present very different views regarding life, death, and suicide. The Greek and later Roman views of suicide were related to their attitudes toward life, death, and freedom. The historian of suicide Henry Romilly Fedden has divided these views roughly into three camps: Pythagoras, Aristotle, and Epicureans were opposed to it, Plato and Socrates took a guarded middle position, and the Stoics and the Cynics accepted it and at times even advocated it.[1]

In his famous dialogue the *Phaedo*, Plato portrays Socrates in his last hours expounding on his views of death. He argues that death frees the soul from the body in order to achieve pure knowledge[2] and return to the far superior world of ideal forms, to which earthly reality is a mere

---

1. Fedden, *Suicide*, 70–85.
2. Plato, *Phaedo*, 66e.

shadow. "The soul is a helpless prisoner chained hand and foot in the body compelled to view reality not directly but only through its prison bars, and wallowing in utter ignorance."[3] Indeed, Socrates argues that philosophy is "preparation for death"[4] and even represents "desire for death.[5]" Given the preference for death over life, it seems only a short step for Socrates to be asked, "Then why not suicide?" Socrates responds with his famous guard-post allegory as an argument against suicide. A person is the property of the gods. Life is a sorry business but we must not leave our guard-post unless we are relieved by the gods.[6]

Aristotle seems less obsessed with the idea of suicide than is Plato and indeed the topic only occupies a few lines in all his extant writings. Aristotle argues that, for certain reasons, suicide is the act of a coward: for example, suicide as an escape from "poverty or disappointed love or bodily or mental anguish is the deed of a coward . . . The suicide braves death not for some noble object but to escape ill."[7]

Aristotle adds that suicide is an injustice against the state, which the state may punish. Unlike Socrates in his *Phaedo* allegory, Aristotle does not mention that humans are the property of the gods, but mentions only obligation to the state. But the man who cuts his own throat in a fit of temper is voluntarily doing an injury that the law does not allow. It follows that the suicide commits an injustice against the state. It is for this reason that the state attaches a penalty, which takes the form of a stigma put on one who has destroyed himself, on the ground that he is guilty of an offense against the state.[8]

3. Ibid., 83a.
4. Ibid., 64a, 68a.
5. Ibid., 64b.
6. Ibid., 62b-c.
7. Aristotle, *Ethics*, 5.11.
8. Durkheim (*Suicide*, 329–32) argues that understanding Aristotle is the key to understanding the Greek laws on suicide. Suicide is illegal when it is not authorized by the state and legal when it is so authorized. In Athens, Cyprus, and Thebes, a suicide was denied regular burial. This rule was even more severe in Sparta (Aeschines, *Speeches: Against Ctesiphon*, 244.8; Plato, *Laws*, 9.12; Dio Chrysostom, *Orations*, 4.14). On the other hand, suicide was tolerated and even assisted when it had received prior state approval. In Athens, as well as in Massilia and Ceos, such a suicide was actually supplied with hemlock (Valerius Maximus, 2, 6.7–8). According to Libanius (quoted by Durkheim), the laws in Athens read as follows: "Whosoever no longer wishes to live shall state his reasons to the Senate; and after having received permission shall abandon life. If your existence is hateful to you, die; if you are overwhelmed by fate, drink the hemlock. If

The equation of suicide with freedom is given most direct expression in the writings of the Greek and Roman Stoics. The Stoic attempts to conquer death by choosing it on his own terms. Zeno, the founder of the Stoic school, defined the goal of life as living in accordance with nature.[9] If this does not occur, suicide becomes the wise choice. Far more important than the particular philosophical spin is the sense that the value of life itself is conditional.

The Stoic feels bound by necessity and seeks a sense of freedom and release. In this area, among others, the philosophy of Stoicism seems to suffer from a sort of constipation. One should escape from this life whenever he chooses, and he should die when the means are at hand: "Choose any part of nature and tell it to let you out."[10] One should pick the means by which to quit life, for the option of suicide leaves the road to freedom open. To grumble is pointless, since life holds no one fast. "Do you like life, then live on. Do you dislike it? Then you're free to return to the place you came from."[11] The philosopher may choose his own mode of death just as he chooses a ship or a house. He leaves life as he would a banquet—when it is time.[12]

In one of the clearest statements of Stoicism, Cicero argues that suicide is inappropriate when a man's circumstances are positive and appropriate when they are negative,[13] and he depicts death as freeing man from chains.[14] Lucius Anneaus Seneca, the brilliant Roman writer and statesman, goes even further, specifically equating suicide with freedom.

> You see that yawning precipice? It leads to liberty. You see that flood, that river, that well? Liberty houses within them. You see that stunted, parched and sorry tree? From each branch, liberty hangs. Your neck, your throat, your heart are so many ways of escape from slavery . . . Do you inquire the road to freedom? You shall find it in every vein of your body.[15]

---

you are bowed with grief, abandon life. Let the unhappy man recount his misfortune, let the magistrate supply him with the remedy, and his wretchedness will come to an end."

9. Diogenes Laertius, *Lives*, 7.87.

10. Seneca, *Epistles*, 117.23–24.

11. Ibid., 70.15.

12. Ibid., 70.11; Plotinus, *On Suicide*, 1.9.

13. Cicero, *De Finibus Bonorum et Malorum*, 3:60.

14. Cicero, *Tusculan Disputations*, 1:18; 1:84

15. Seneca, *De Ira*, 3.15.3–4.

Seneca and his wife Paulina put these thoughts into action, methodi-
cally cutting their wrists at the order of his former pupil, the emperor Nero.[16]

Thus was the suicidal pessimism of Greek thought and law carried
into Roman society as well. When the second-century philosopher Lucian realized that he was no longer able to take care of himself, he declared: "Here endeth a contest awarding the fairest of prizes: time calls,
and forbids us delay." Then, refraining from all food, he took his leave
of life in his habitual cheerful humor. A short time before the end, he
was asked, "What orders have you to give about your burial?" He replied:
"Don't borrow trouble! The stench will get me buried."[17]

This preoccupation with suicide has received more recent expression in both the famous soliloquy of Shakespeare's *Hamlet*: "To be or not
to be, that is the question . . . "[18] And in Albert Camus's *The Myth of
Sisyphus:* "There is but one truly serious philosophical problem, and that
is suicide."[19]

The biblical view of suicide is entirely different. The choice between
life and death is not one to mull over daily, as talk of suicide so fills the letters of Seneca and other writings of classical philosophers. Suicide is forbidden in the Torah (Hebrew Scriptures). It is possible to derive an injunction
against suicide from the Noahide laws: "For your lifeblood too, I will require a reckoning."[20] This statement has been seen as a prohibition not only
against suicide but also against any form of self-mutilation.[21] The Hebrew
Bible contains several additional prohibitions regarding self-mutilation,
for example: "Ye are the children of the Lord your God: Ye shall not cut

---

16. Suicide is not specifically mentioned in the fragments of the Roman law of the
Twelve Tables. Nevertheless, several later sources note the refusals to allow suicides to
be buried and even of the crucifixion of their corpses (Pliny, *Natural History,* 36.24).
Quintilian, however, claims that the ban on suicide could be lifted in certain cases, given
prior approval by the Senate (Quintilian, *Inst. Orat.,* 7.4.39). Motives were important in
Roman law. For example, suicide was not punishable if caused by "impatience of pain or
sickness" or "weariness of life, lunacy or fear of dishonor" (Justinian, *Digest,* 48.21.3.6).
These laws tended to reflect both the earlier Aristotelian concept that humans were possessions of the state and the suicidal pessimism of the later Roman Stoics.

17. *Lucian on Demonax,* 65, 66.

18. Shakespeare, *Hamlet,* 3.1.55–75.

19. Camus, *Myth of Sisyphus,* 3.

20. Gen 9:5.

21. *b. Baba Kamma* 91b.

yourselves, nor make any baldness between your eyes for the dead."[22] Much the same prohibition is given specifically to the priests in Leviticus: "They shall not make baldness upon their head, neither shall they shave off the corners of their beard, nor make any cuttings in their flesh."[23]

But perhaps more important than a prohibition against suicide is the biblical enhancement and promotion of life. God has given the Torah to human beings as a guide for living, not as a preparation for death. "Ye shall therefore keep my statutes, and mine ordinances, which if a man do, he shall live in them: I am the Lord."[24] The human being is commanded to choose life: "See, I have put before you today life and death, blessing and curse, and you shall choose life so that you and your seed shall live."[25]

The biblical position is to promote life, not simply to prevent suicide. Death *per se* is never a desired solution in the biblical traditions. The biblical mindset has a very different view of freedom and the relationship between body and soul. The Mishna (Oral Torah) is not concerned with fate and real freedom always exists in the human realm, i.e., the freedom to act righteously. However, the Mishna does not posit illusory freedom or choice in matters beyond human control. In this way the rabbis are the polar opposites of the Stoics. Where the Stoics felt overwhelmed by necessity or fate in all things except in the time and manner of death, the rabbis argued that in such matters as death, there is in fact, no choice. "Against your will you are born, against it you shall in the future give account before the King of Kings."[26]

Biblical man acknowledges God's total power over birth, life, and death. In so doing he accepts the responsibility of his freedom to make moral choices. Birth and death are events beyond human understanding that God alone will handle. The individual is given freedom in terms of following God's commandments. Freedom can be achieved only in the acceptance of the realities of man's relationship with God. The Mishna offers its own statement on freedom. Playing with biblical Hebrew, the Mishna states the Ten Commandments were carved (*harut*) on stone. "Read not *harut* (carved) but *herut* (freedom). One is not free unless he

22. Deut 14:1.
23. Lev 21:5.
24. Lev 18:5.
25. Deut 30:19.
26. *b. Avot* 4:29.

devotes himself to study of the Torah."[27] This sets the stage for a striking psychological contrast. For Greeks and Romans, suicide represents a very high form of creativity. In Judaism, life itself is the essence of creativity and suicide only destroys this opportunity. In response to bad news (e.g., a death, a natural disaster, a tragedy), an observant Jew says the blessing: *Baruch Dyan HaEmeth* (Blessed is the true judge).

The Stoic comparison of life to a banquet from which one may depart at will meets a striking antithesis in a second-century Mishnaic statement: "This world is like a portico before the world to come. Prepare yourself in the portico so that you may enter into the banquet hall."[28] That is, prepare yourself in this world by living righteously so that you may merit the rewards of the next world. The two worlds are dissimilar in function: in this world, good deeds and repentance are appropriate and more beautiful than all the rewards of the next world; at the same time, the peace of spirit attainable in the next world is preferable to all of the joys of this world. Therefore, earthly life is not a banquet that must inevitably end. It is a time for work and preparation. The contrast with Stoic views carries on to a second point: one must not assume that the next world is some sort of refuge from this one.[29] There is still awareness, and one must come before the King of Kings for a final judgment that will be beyond anything earthly people can comprehend. Both earth and heaven are thus important, but each in its own way.

Freedom here means freedom of the human spirit from fears and desires. When our fears and desires run wanton then they dominate us and there is no freedom. The Rabbinic Jew acknowledges God's total power over birth, life, and death. In so doing he accepts the responsibility of his freedom to make moral choices. Birth and death are events beyond human understanding that God alone will handle. The individual is given freedom in terms of following God's commandments.

Greek Narratives

As can be seen in Table 1, some eighteen suicide attempts, self-mutilations, and completed suicides occur in the twenty-six extant plays of two Greek playwrights, Euripides and Sophocles. The great sociologist,

27. Ibid., 6:2.
28. Ibid., 4:21–22.
29. Ibid., 4.

Émile Durkheim[30] distinguished three types of suicides: *egoistic* suicides resulting from a lack of connection between self and society, *altruistic* suicides resulting from a lack of differentiation between self and society, and *anomic* suicides, referring to a confusion in boundaries between self and society. Most of the Euripides' suicides are altruistic in this sense, while most of those in Sophocles' tragedies are egoistic.

Table 1: Suicide Narratives in Greek Tragedy

Character	Gender	Source (Playwright)	Method	Type
Phaedra	F	*Hippolytus* (Euripides)	Stabbing	Anomic
Menoe-ceus	M	*The Phoenissae* (Euripides)	Jumping	Altruistic
Jocasta	F	*The Phoenissae* (Euripides)	Stabbing	Altruistic
Evadne	F	*The Suppliants* (Euripides)	Burning	Anomic
Alcestis	F	*Alcestis* (Euripides)	Unspecified	Altruistic
Macaria	F	*The Heracleidae* (Euripides)	Stabbing	Altruistic
Polyxena	F	*Hecuba* (Euripides)	Stabbing	Altruistic
Iphigenia	F	*Iphigenia in Aulis* (Euripides)	Stabbing	Altruistic
Jocasta	F	*Oedipus Rex* (Sophocles)	Hanging	Egoistic
Oedipus	M	*Oedipus Rex* (Sophocles)	Self-blinding	Anomic
Antigone	F	*Antigone* (Sophocles)	Hanging	Anomic
Haemon	M	*Antigone* (Sophocles)	Stabbing	Egoistic
Eurydice	F	*Antigone* (Sophocles)	Stabbing	Egoistic
Deianeira	F	*The Trachinae* (Sophocles)	Stabbing	Anomic
Heracles	M	*The Trachinae* (Sophocles)	Burning	Egoistic
Ajax	M	*Ajax* (Sophocles)	Stabbing	Egoistic

As can be seen in Table 1, suicides occur in seven of Euripides' surviving plays: *Hippolytus, The Phoenissae, The Suppliants, Alcestis, The*

---

30. Durkheim, *Suicide.*

Hericleidae, Hecuba, and *Iphigenia in Aulis.* Most of these suicides are women, and they fall into a pattern of ritual murder, in which the protagonist does not actually raise a hand against herself, but allows herself to be sacrificed.

In *Hippolytus,* Phaedra, the wife of King Theseus of Athens, hangs herself after being caused, by the goddess Aphrodite's design, to fall madly in love with her misogynistic, vain, and moralistic stepson, Hippolytus. Though she resists her passion, with great misery to herself, her servant betrays her secret to raping her.[31] Phaedra is left alone, then hangs herself, leaving behind a note that falsely accuses Hippolytus of raping her. Phaedra destroys herself because, much like Sophocles' Antigone, she is embedded in a miserable situation. At the same time, she has an unrealistic expectation of herself. Vacillating between the altruistic and egoistic positions leads Phaedra to an anomic suicide.

The Phoenissae portrays two suicides, Menoeceus, Creon's son, and Jocasta, both altruistic. The seer Tiresias informs the Thebans that the city can be saved from the invaders only by the death of a young unmarried man. Menoeceus stabs himself, genuinely believing that he must give precedence to the city over his own private needs and indeed his own life. The second suicide, Jocasta, is portrayed by Euripides as stabbing herself out of grief and a sense of impotence after failing to prevent her two sons, Eteocles and Polyneices, from killing each other, fulfilling their father Oedipus's curse.[32]

In *The Suppliants,* Evadne kills herself by jumping on the funeral pyre of her husband Theseus. Evadne is not caught up in an inescapable destructive environment. Rather, her largely personal problems impel her to jump onto the funeral pyre of her husband. Morbid and depressed, she is "resolved not to save her life, or to prove untrue to her husband."[33] She seeks some recognition or notice, especially from her father, and will "leap from this rack in honor's cause."[34] Perhaps her father's indifference is the root of Evadne's anomic behavior and her suicide as she vacillates erratically between a desire for symbiosis and a desire for recognition.

---

31. Euripides, *Hippolytus*, lines 347–783.
32. Euripides, *Phoenissae*, lines 1–168, 935–1040, 1204–8, 1281–82, 1449–453.
33. Euripides, *Suppliants*, line 1024–31.
34. Ibid., 1015.

The remaining four Euripidean suicides are the clearest altruistic types, where a heroine kills herself for the good of someone else or for a larger societal need. In *Alcestis*, King Admetus of Thessaly is told that the Fates demand his death unless he can find someone who is willing to die in his place. Admetus's aged parents sharply refuse his request, but Alcestis, his young and beautiful wife, kills herself in his place.[35] In the opening scene, a god (Death) meets Apollo in a deadly serious debate for the life of Alcestis. Humans do not really have a right to enjoy their life on the earth: who they are or what they have accomplished means nothing. In the end, the netherworld makes demands, and all of this means that one of the characters must die. Alcestis is the one who will satisfy Death's claims.

The Heracleidae begins after the death of Heracles. Afterwards, his family seeks refuge in Athens from his old enemy, King Eurystheus of Argos, who wishes to kill them. Demophon of Athens is willing to help the fugitives, but an oracle pronounces that a girl of noble descent must be sacrificed to the goddess Persephone in order for him to defeat the Argives. Heracles' daughter Macaria learns of the trouble from Iolaus, her father's old friend, and she seems to take total responsibility by offering herself as the victim. Iolaus is greatly moved by Macaria's altruistic gesture, praising her as a true daughter of Heracles. He suggests a fairer method, a lottery involving Macaria and her sisters, but Macaria will have none of this. Her sacrifice for others has no meaning if it is imposed through a lottery. "My death shall no chance lot decide, there is no graciousness in that peace, old friend. But if ye accept and will avail you of my readiness, freely do I offer my life for those, and without constraint."[36]

She echoes the words of the stoic Seneca discussed in chapter 8, saying that one fulfills one's purpose in life most fully by the way one leaves it: "For I, by loving not my life too well have found a treasure very fair, a glorious means to leave it."[37] This wins the approval of those around her.[38] Through her self-sacrifice, Macaria fulfills the way of her father, Heracles.[39] This seems to be the epitome of altruistic suicide: Macaria must die

---

35. Euripides, *Alcestis*, line 394.
36. Euripides, *Heracleidae*, lines 541–43.
37. Ibid., 532–33.
38. Ibid., 534–39.
39. Ibid., 563–64.

to fulfill her father's glory, but she must have the heroic sense that she has chosen it freely.

Euripides' *Hecuba* describes the sacrifice of Polyxena, prisoner of the Greek conquerors after the fall of Troy and the last surviving daughter of Queen Hecuba and King Priam. The play commences with the Greek fleet ready to return home after sacking Troy. The ghost of Achilles appears and demands that a Trojan virgin be sacrificed on his tomb before the fleet can sail. The Greeks vote that the virgin to be sacrificed is Polyxena. What is so telling is her reaction. First, there is Polyxena's sense of ruin and outrage: "For my own life, its ruin and its outrage, never a tear shed; nay death is become to me a happier lot than life."[40] Then, however is her insistence that her death is a heroic act, and indeed voluntary. Indeed, she prefers death to unheroic behavior. Rather than rebuke her executioners for murdering her, she forgives them. Like Macaria, she seeks to create the illusion of control over her own death: "Of my free will I die; let none lay hand on me; for bravely will I yield my neck."[41] The Greeks are impressed with the bravery of their Trojan captive, and they unbind her. Polyxena then voluntarily tears open her robe, sinks to her knee, and bares her breast. Her heroic sense of noblesse oblige leads her on to altruistic suicide: "Young prince, if 'tis my breast thou'dst strike, lo! here it is, strike home! or if at my neck thy sword thou'lt aim, behold! that neck is bared."[42] From Polyxena's point of view, this becomes altruistic suicide, or martyrdom. She needs to feel that she is dying freely because she cannot confront her captors with their injustice.

Iphigenia in Aulis portrays Euripides' final suicide, that of Iphigenia, daughter of Agamemnon, which may be the most poignant and illustrative of all of Euripides' altruistic suicides. Iphigenia, following the pattern described above of Macaria and Polyxena, accepts willingly, almost gladly, a seer's order that she must be sacrificed before her father's army will be able to sail for Troy. This is the gold standard for ritual murder, not suicide in the contemporary use of the word; however, in this play there is no real distinction.

The play's characters are encumbered with the same problem as so many other characters of Greek drama—the general cheapness of human life in the heroic view of man. Agamemnon laments: "Woe, woe is me.

40. Euripides, *Hecuba*, lines 210–11.
41. Ibid., 559–62.
42. Ibid., 570–72.

97

Unhappy, caught by fate, outwitted by the cunning of the gods."[43] Nevertheless, Agamemnon still feels compelled to kill Iphigenia, even when his brother Menelaus relents in his demands for her sacrifice. Indeed, Iphigenia herself seems to avoid any active attempt to evade her death. Rather, she grasps for a freedom that she does not have by trying to make her death seem voluntary instead of obligatory: "I have chosen death: it is my own free choice. I have put cowardice away from me. Honor is mine now. O mother, say I am right."[44] It seems normal to Iphigenia that she should die in a heroic attempt to help the army and thereby salve her father's feelings, win his approval, and fulfill her family's tradition. This negation of self shows Iphigenia's suicide to be altruistic. She is unable to free herself from the group pressure around her.

Suicide is a major theme in four of Sophocles' seven surviving plays as well: *Oedipus Rex, Antigone, Ajax,* and *The Trachinae.* These are different than the suicides in Euripides. Most of these figures are male, and also are portrayed as actively taking their own lives rather than have the act forced upon them by others.

Oedipus Rex contains one egoistic suicide (Jocasta) and one anomic self-mutilation (Oedipus himself). Jocasta hangs herself when the tragic truth of her incestuous relationship with her son Oedipus is revealed. Oedipus rushes into the palace determined to murder his mother-wife Jocasta, but when he discovers that she has hung herself, he plunges the golden brooch she was wearing into his eyes, blinding himself.[45]

Sophocles' *Antigone* contains three suicides, those of Antigone (anomic), Haemon (egoistic), and Eurydice (egoistic). Antigone is the daughter of the incestuous union of Oedipus and Jocasta, and has buried her murdered brother Polyneices (see chapter 7 on the curse of Oedipus) against the order of her uncle Creon. Creon responds by burying Antigone alive. She hangs herself, mimicking the death of her mother Jocasta. Haemon, the son of Creon, and Antigone's would-be suitor, falls on his sword after finding her dead, after first attempting unsuccessfully to stab his father Creon. Finally, Eurydice, the wife of Creon and mother

---

43. Euripides, *Iphigenia in Aulis*, lines 442–45.

44. Ibid., 1375–77.

45. Sophocles, *Oedipus Rex*, lines 1261–70.

of Haemon, stabs herself upon learning of her son's suicide, blaming her husband.[46]

Two more suicides occur in Sophocles' *The Trachiniae*—the anomic self-stabbing of Deianeira, the abandoned wife of Heracles, and Heracles' own egoistic self-burning on a pyre. When Deianeira learns Heracles has abandoned her for Iole, has sends Heracles a robe dipped in the blood of a centaur that Heracles had previously slain. On a conscious level, Deianera thinks this robe will serve as a charm to win her husband's love back to her. Unconsciously, the robe expresses her fury, bursting into fire and sticking to his Heracles' skin, causing him great agony. When Deianera realizes what she has done, she offers no expression of sympathy or remorse towards Heracles, but stabs herself in her own marriage bed, presumably the same bed Heracles intends to share with Iole.[47] Heracles, in agony rushes to kill Deianeira. Only after Heracles learns that Deianeira has already killed herself does he ask his son Hyllus to throw him on a burning pyre, because he is now too incapacitated to carry out the act himself.[48]

Perhaps the gold standard of an egoistic suicide is that of the great Greek warrior Ajax in Sophocles' play of the same name. Ajax has gone mad with jealousy because Achilles' armor has been given to Odysseus; so, in a frenzied state, he tries to murder Odysseus. The goddess Athena prevents him from doing so by deflecting his anger so that he slaughters a herd of sheep instead. The text makes clear that Athena not only wants to restrain Ajax but to humiliate him deeply as well, and to mock him in his madness in front of Odysseus. Ajax's hubris has provoked Athena's anger. The very intensity of Athena's wrath sets the stage for Ajax's subsequent self-stabbing. As his rage passes, it is replaced by a self-destructive depression, which is not uncommon among egoistic suicides:

His defenses are overcome, and he cries for the first time, refusing food or drink. Ajax first contemplates murdering Odysseus, and then himself. Ajax's suicidal aims are even more clearly articulated in his ruminations about his lost honor in the eyes of his father. An honorable suicide becomes in his eyes his only solution. The need for his mother's attention appears in Ajax's daydream of her grief at his death: "She, woeful woman,

---

46. Sophocles, Antigone, lines 947–1292

47. Sophocles, *Trachinae*, lines 524–892.

48. Ibid., 1193–96.

when she hears these tidings will wail out a large dirge through the entire town."[49] Immediately after this refrain, Ajax falls on his sword and dies.[50]

It is the reaction of others to Ajax's depression on which we wish to focus. Ajax's friends do not know how to deal with his problem. He certainly does not disguise his suicidal intent, yet those around him allow him to go off by himself, which is clearly not recommended for suicide prevention. In fact, Ajax's brother, Teucer, is the only one to take a step toward suicide prevention: he sends a messenger from the Greek chieftains ordering that Ajax not be left alone.[51] The messenger arrives too late, but the common sense suicide-preventive message is clear: Do not leave a suicidally depressed person alone!

A number of points stand out in these great but tragic Greek plays.

1. Life is ultimately tragic, with no hope of redemption. Heroic suicide and self-sacrifice offer a meaning for these people not available in life.

2. Greek figures are unable to develop a healthy view of themselves in society. People cannot really change, but only cycle back and forth between suicidal polarities. Either they are altruistic (e.g., Euripides' Iphigenia) or egoistic (Sophocles' Ajax) or anomically split between the two (Sophocles' Antigone). Characters seek individuation at the expense of attachment, and attachment at the expense of individuation. Suicide is the all-too-frequent result.

3. Often, protagonists are totally isolated from their surrounds (Ajax) or urged or even compelled to let them be sacrificed for a larger goal. Some (e.g., Macaria, Polxyena and Iphigenia) attempt to convert an involuntary sentence imposed upon them into a voluntary act of self-destruction.

4. There is no attempt to intervene to prevent other characters (e.g., Ajax) from committing suicide. Ajax is left alone, without human company or any offer of simple comforts such as food or drink.

49. Sophocles, *Ajax*, lines 848–49.

50. Ibid, 855–64.

51. Ibid., 795–96.

Biblical Narratives

There are only six suicides in the entire Hebrew Bible and none in the Pentateuch (see Table 2). Chronologically, they are as follows: the self-stabbing of Abimelech,[52] the crushing of Samson,[53] the self-stabbing of Saul and his armor bearer,[54] the hanging of Ahitophel,[55] and the burning of Zimri.[56] They are listed in Table 2. Here we add an additional suicidal type to that postulated by Durkheim—a *covenantal* suicide type which is neither egoistic, altruistic, or anomic, but which is done for a higher purpose in which the individual acts as a developed personality who is part of a larger goal, in this case the covenantal framework of the people of Israel itself.

Table 2: Suicide Narratives in the Hebrew Bible

Character	Gender	Source	Method	Type
Ahitophel	M	2 Sam 17:23	Strangled	Egoistic
Zimri	M	1 Kgs 16:18	Burning	Egoistic
Ahimelech	M	Judg 9:54	Sword	Egoistic
Samson	M	Judg 16:30	Being Crushed	Covenantal
Saul	M	1 Sam 31:4; 2 Sam 1:6; 1 Chr 10:4	Sword	Covenantal
Saul's Armor-Bearer	M	1 Sam 31:5; 1 Chron. 10:5	Sword	Altruistic

Ahitophel, a counselor of King David, has joined Absalom's rebellion against David. But when he perceives that Absalom has been tricked into following a foolhardy plan that is certain to lead to David's victory, Ahitophel sets his house in order and strangles himself.[57] Several reasons, all egoistic, have probably prompted Ahitophel's suicide. First, he now

52. Judg 9:54.
53. Judg 16:30.
54. 1 Sam 31:14–15; 2 Sam 1:6; 1 Chr 10:4–5.
55. 2 Sam 17:23.
56. 1 Kgs 16:18.
57. 2 Sam 17:23.

fears that Absalom's attempt to overthrow David is doomed and that he will die a traitor's death. Second, and less likely, is Ahitophel's disgust at Absalom's conduct in setting aside his counsel, which has wounded Ahitophel's pride and disappointed his ambition. Third, David's curse may have prompted Ahitophel to hang himself.[58] Finally, rabbinic writers have also argued that, since Ahitophel is a suicide, his family inherits his estate. If he were to be executed as a rebel, his possessions would be forfeited to the king. Ahitophel is listed in the Mishna[59] as among those who have forfeited their share in the world to come.

The wicked Zimri is also an egoistic suicide. King Elah of Israel passes his days drinking in his palace while his warriors battle the Philistines. Zimri, a high-ranking officer, takes advantage of this situation, assassinates Elah, and mounts the throne. His reign, however, lasts only seven days. As soon as the news of King Elah's murder reaches the army on the battlefield, they pronounce General Omri to be king and lay siege to the palace. When Zimri sees that he is unable to hold out against the siege, he sets fire to the palace and perishes in the flames: "And it came to pass, when Zimri saw that the city was taken that he went into the castle of the king's house, and burnt the king's house over him with fire, and he died."[60]

Abimelech's suicide is, strictly speaking, an assisted suicide. After carving out a principality for himself in Israel by means of various brutalities, he is mortally wounded by a millstone that a woman throws from a fortress she is besieging. Realizing that he is dying, Abimelech asks his armor-bearer to finish him off so that it will not be said that a woman has killed him. This act of hubris qualifies him as an egoistic suicide.[61]

Now we come to three more sympathetic biblical suicides: Samson, Saul, and Saul's armor bearer. Samson, the great defender and leader of the Israelites, had been blinded and publicly mocked by the Philistines. Faced with torture and death, he asked God for the strength to take as many Philistines with him as possible; when granted his request, he pulled down the central pillars of the temple of Dagon, killing thousands in one last blow:

58. *b. Makkot* 4a.
59. *b. Sanhedrin* 10:2.
60. 1 Kings 16:18.
61. Judg 9:53–57.

> Strengthen me, I pray, just this once . . . And Samson took hold
> of the two middle pillars which supported the temple, and braced
> himself against them, one on his right and the other on his left.
> Then Samson said, "Let me die with the Philistines."[62]

It is tempting to see Samson as the biblical equivalent of Sophocles'
Ajax. Samson, like Ajax, has fallen from his previous state of leadership.
Is he, too, using suicide to restore his lost image in the eyes of others?
Closer examination indicates that Samson's suicide is not egoistic like
that of Ajax: he is not alienated from his society but is very much a part
of the people of Israel. Is Samson's suicide, therefore, altruistic and self-
sacrificing? We must also reject this interpretation. Samson does not suffer from a failing sense of his own personality; rather, he calls on God to
strengthen him in his final attempt to destroy the Philistines. His purpose
is not self-annihilation but the carrying out of his divinely ordained mission to free Israel from the Philistines. Samson's suicide thus seems to be
neither egoistic nor altruistic; rather, it may be labeled covenantal in the
sense that it is in the service of the biblical God, with neither over isolation nor over-integration in his boundaries with his society. Significantly,
his final action in life leads to a long period of peace.[63]

A second covenantal suicide is that of King Saul. Rabbinic literature
has regarded King Saul as a man of great stature, the anointed of the Lord.
Yet his reign was marked by series of mistakes, ending with his own suicide during a losing battle against the Philistines on Mount Gilboa. Saul
has seen three of his sons and many of his fighters slain, and he himself is
severely wounded. Surrounded by enemies and not wishing to be taken
prisoner and exposed to the mockery and brutality of the Philistines,
King Saul entreats his armor-bearer to kill him. The latter refuses and
Saul falls on his own sword: "Then Saul said to his armor-bearer: 'Draw
your sword, and thrust me through with it, lest these uncircumcised men
come and thrust me through and abuse me.' But his armor-bearer would
not, for he was greatly afraid. Therefore Saul took a sword, and fell on it."[64]

The suicide of Saul has been taken by commentators in different ways.
The Midrash Rabbah[65] has pointed to Saul as an example of a permissible

62. Judg 16:28–30.

63. Judg 13.

64. 1 Sam 31:4.

65. *Midrash Genesis Rabbah* 9:5. See also *Midrash Rabbah,* 34:13, and *Shulchan Aruch, Yoreh Deah* 345:3.

suicide. One commentator has considered Saul as a special case because, before the final battle with the Philistines, he received a message from the witch of Endor that he would die. Thus, by taking his own life, he is not defying Providence. Other commentators have viewed Saul as an example of a suicide who takes his own life in order to avoid greater profanation of the divine name. In this view, Saul fears that if he is captured alive by the Philistines, they will desecrate his body, either by torture or by forcing him to commit idolatrous acts. This interpretation means that suicide may be permissible if it is committed in order to prevent dishonor to God's name rather than for personal reasons. As such, Saul's suicide can be classified as covenantal rather than as either egoistic or altruistic.

The suicide of Saul's armor-bearer can be classified as altruistic because of his seeming lack of differentiation from Saul: "And when his armor-bearer saw that Saul was dead, he also fell on his sword, and died with him."[66] The biblical passage tells us that the armor-bearer first refuses to kill Saul and then falls on his own sword in response to Saul's suicide. The most sympathetic rabbinic treatment is given to the covenantal suicides (Samson and Saul). The harshest judgments are applied to suicides that seem clearly egoistic (Ahitophel, Zimri, and Abimelech).

One suicide occurs in the Christian New Testament—the self-hanging of Judas Iscariot.[67] There are several suicides occurring in the non-rabbinic writings of the Second Temple period as well. In the apocryphal book of 1 Maccabees, for example, Eleazar sacrifices himself by darting beneath the elephant of an enemy general and running his sword into it.[68] In the book of 2 Maccabees, two acts of suicide are recorded: first, that of Ptolemy, and second, that of Ragesh (Razis). Ptolemy, an advocate of the Judeans at the Syrian Court of King Antiochus Eupator, poisons himself after being accused of treason.[69] Ragesh first attempts unsuccessfully to die on his sword rather than fall into the hands of the Syrians. He subsequently succeeds in disemboweling himself after throwing himself from a wall.[70] The historian Flavius Josephus also mentions a number of suicides in his work *Wars of the Jews,* including the mass suicides at Jotapata in

---

66. 1 Sam 31:5.

67. Matt 27:5; Acts 1:18.

68. 1 Macc 6:46.

69. 2 Macc 10:12.

70. 2 Macc 14:41–46.

69 CE and Masada in 73 CE.[71] There are a few cases of suicide reported in the Talmud as well, often in response to persecutions,[72] and two more suicides are mentioned in the *Midrash Rabbah*.[73]

Nevertheless, no Talmudic passage can be taken as praising suicide or glorifying heroism in the Greek sense, nor is martyrdom sought for its own sake. For example, the Romans tortured Rabbi Akiba cruelly when they found him teaching the Torah during the period of persecution that followed the Bar Kochba War (135 CE) As the story is told in the Babylonian Talmud,[74] a Roman officer saw Rabbi Akiba smiling and asked him why. Rabbi Akiba responded that he was in great agony and he knew that he would soon die. He was only happy that, in his last moment, he could still sanctify God's name by reciting the Shema prayer: "Hear oh Israel, the Lord our God is one." Rabbi Akiba did not seek martyrdom and felt no beatific joy in his pain; rather, he continued to express his faith in God. Note how different this is from the acts of some of Euripides' altruistic suicides (Macaria, Polyxena, and Iphigenia) to pretend their ordered sacrifices were voluntary.

Of most interest to the present chapter are the numbers of cases presented in Table 3 of suicide prevention, which involved individuals who expressed suicidal wishes but were saved by a divine therapeutic intervention (Rebecca, Moses, Jeremiah, Jonah, Job, David, and Elijah). The Bible portrays God as intervening, much as a good therapist might, to deflect the death wishes uttered by one biblical character or another. Two themes stand in marked contrast to Greek literature: first, the biblical characters are not typically under pressure to make a decision that will destroy them; second, the biblical God provides a stopper by offering the characters a chance to overcome their problems.

71. Josephus, *Complete Works*.

72. b. *Tosefot Avodah Zarah* 18a; *Maharsha, Avodah Zarah* 18a; *Sifre* and *Yalkut Shimoni* on Deut 32:4; *Gittin* 57b, *Lamentations Rabbah* 1:45; *Avodah* 18b; *Baba Batra* 3b; *Taanit* 29a; *Hullin* 94a; *Berachot* 23a; *Semachot* 2; 5.

73. See *Ecclesiastes Rabbah* 10:7; *Genesis Rabbah* 65:22.

74. b. *Berachot* 61b.

Table 3: Suicide Prevention Narratives in the Hebrew Bible

Character	Gender	Source	Method of Prevention
Rebecca	F	Genesis 27–28	Appropriate Matchmaking for Son
Moses	M	Numbers 11	Support from Others
Jeremiah	M	Jeremiah	Punishment of Evil
Jonah	M	Jonah	Protected Withdrawal and Guidance
Job	M	Job	Renewal of Relationship
David	M	Psalm 22	Renewal of Faith
Elijah	M	1 Kings 18–19	Rest and Nurturance

After participating in the deception by which they have obtained Isaac's blessing, Rebecca sends Jacob away to his Uncle Laban so that an angry Esau won't kill him. Immediately afterward, Rebecca tells Isaac that her life has been made miserable by Esau's Hittite wives, and she worries that Jacob may marry similarly. Rebecca's words seem more like a message of despair to her husband. Isaac listens to his wife and involves God as a stopper in his command that Jacob not marry one of the daughters of Canaan, who are so offensive to Rebecca. Instead, Jacob marries a daughter of Laban, a kinsman. Rebecca is presumably satisfied, and there is no more mention of her "suicidal" musings.[75]

Deeply disappointed about the complaints of the Israelites, Moses cries out to God that the responsibilities of leading the people are too great and that God should kill him:

> So Moses said to the Lord, "Why have You afflicted Your servant? And why have I not found favor in your sight, that you have laid the burden of all these people on me? . . . I am not able to bear all these people alone, because the burden is too heavy for me. If You

---

75. Gen 27:42–46; 28:1–4.

treat me like this, please kill me here and now—if I have found favor in Your sight—and do not let me see my wretchedness!"[76]

God, the divine therapist, does listen and intervenes with a positive and practical solution. Let Moses select seventy elders to help him lead the Israelites.[77]

Jeremiah expresses a keen disappointment with the evil and suffering he sees around him. In the Book of Jeremiah, the prophet speaks of his disappointment with life in the most uncompromising terms.

> Cursed be the day in which I was born!
> Let the day not be blessed in which my mother bore me!
> Let it not be blessed! . . .
> Why did I come forth from the womb
> To see labor and sorrow,
> That my days should be consumed with shame?[78]

These are the thoughts of a very sensitive man who is disillusioned. Yet he is protected by his faith, and there is no indication that he thinks of suicide. His belief that God will punish evil comes across clearly in the directly preceding passage:

> Sing to the Lord!
> Praise the Lord!
> For He has delivered the soul of the poor
> From the hand of evil-doers. [79]

The suicide prevention of Jonah has been described at length in chapter 2. Jonah is confused and conflicted several times during the narrative. In fact, he expresses the desire to die on several occasions, and event attempts to take his life, first by asking his shipmates to throw him into the sea on his way to Tarshish, and again sitting under a blazing sun, angry that he had warned the people of Nineveh of their wickedness—but he does not commit suicide. In each case, God saves Jonah, first by swallowing him in the belly of a big fish, and second by shielding him with a

---

76. Num 11:11–15.

77. Num. 11:16–19.

78. Jer 20:14–18.

79. Jer 20:13.

gourd. In each case God as the divine therapist enables Jonah to regroup and find his way forward.[80]

The book of Job is one of the most challenging in the entire Hebrew Bible. We will compare the story of Job to Zeno in chapter 10. Let us summarize it here with regard to God's role in preventing Job's suicide: A just man, Job is assailed by a series of awesome misfortunes—the loss of his wealth, his family, and his health. Further his friends turn against him, questioning his innocence and even his wife urges him to "curse God and die." Job rebukes her, saying: "What, shall we receive good at the hand of God, and shall we not receive evil?"[81]

Job is deeply grieved by these events, but his existential faith in God and life is not destroyed. Job does express what a modern suicidologist might interpret as a threat of suicide: "So that my soul chooseth strangling and death rather than these my bones. I loathe it; I shall not live always. Let me alone; for my days are vanity."[82] Still, what Job is really interested in is a reaffirmation of his relationship with God.

Job maintains his innocence in his suffering refusing to be silent and again he expresses the weariness of his life while he calls on God for meaning: "My soul is weary of my life." Even so, he again refuses to be silent: "I will say to God, 'Do not condemn me; show me why You contend with me.'" Job finds strength in his faith: "Though He slay me, yet will I trust Him." Indeed, he will continue to trust God no matter what God does to him. He asks only that God maintain an open relationship with him: "Then call, and I will answer; or let me speak, then You respond to me."[83] Beginning in Job 38, God does speak directly to Job, confirming the importance of their continuing relationship and God's care for his creation. Even though Job cannot understand God's ways, he continues his love for him. And this sense of being loved even through misfortune sustains Job.

David too exhibits despair, abandonment and even suicidal thoughts in some of his psalms, but the psalmist renews his faith in God and overcomes these feelings of heavy self-doubt. An example of this process can

---

80. Jonah 1:11–16; 2:1; 4:1–6.
81. Job 2:9–31.
82. Job 7:15–16.
83. Job 9:21; 10:1–2; 13: 15, 22.

be seen in the famous Psalm 22. It begins in despair over the psalmist's perception of his complete and utter abandonment by God.

> My God, my God, why have You forsaken me?
> Why are You so far from helping me,
> and from the words of my groaning?
> O my God, I cry in the daytime, but You do not hear. . . [84]

Indeed, the first verse of this psalm is cited in the Gospel of Matthew as the last thing Jesus said as he was dying on the cross.[85] Psalm 22 continues with the psalmist's return to the roots of his faith—to the earliest stages of trust.[86] He overcomes the reproach of mockers and recovers his faith and thus overcomes his despair.

> But You are He who took me out of the womb;
> You made me trust while on my mother's breasts.
> I was cast upon You from birth,
> From my mother's womb You have been my God.[87]

God provides the stopper. He has been the rock of the psalmist's faith since the primal experiences of birth and nursing. This basic trust that the psalmist has established with God is sufficient to overcome the psalmist's doubts and fears of abandonment:

> Nor has He hidden His face from him;
> But when he cried to Him, He heard.[88]

Perhaps the gold standard of a suicide prevention story in the Hebrew Bible is that of the prophet Elijah. It is profound yet very simple and practical. The story begins with Elijah reaching a peak of triumph when he gains a stunning moral and political victory over the priests of Baal in their confrontation on Mount Carmel.[89] Even King Ahab supports Elijah, and now God has sent rain to end the long drought in Israel. However, Queen Jezebel, Ahab's Phoenician wife, remains recalcitrant. She threatens to kill Elijah, and he flees for his life to the desert of Be'er Sheva. There he sits alone under a bush and asks God to take away his life.

84. Ps 22:1–3.
85. Matt 27:46.
86. See Erikson, *Identity, Youth and Crisis*.
87. Ps 22:9–11.
88. Ps 22:24.
89. 1 Kgs 18:41.

> But he himself went a day's journey into the wilderness, and came and sat down under a broom tree. And he prayed that he might die, and said, "It is enough! Now, Lord, take my life, for I am no better than my fathers!"[90]

Elijah is exhausted and deeply disappointed at the failure that has followed so soon after his moment of seeming victory. He falls into despair, questioning the very value of his own life. Unlike Ajax, Elijah is not left alone in his depression and demoralization. God treats his suicidal outburst as a call for help. As the divine therapist, God pays attention and arranges for practical hands-on help. God first provides rest for Elijah; then, unlike Sophocles' Ajax or Euripides' Phaedra, an angel of God twice provides him with food and drink, preparing him for the work that remains to be done.

> Then as he lay and slept under a broom tree, suddenly an angel touched him, and said to him: "Arise and eat" . . . So he arose, and ate and drank; and he went on the strength of that food forty days and forty nights as far as Horeb, the mountain of God.[91]

Showing consideration for others by giving them food shows up several times in the biblical account about Elijah. God sends Elijah food, carried by ravens, from the table of King Asa of Judah. Elijah also saves the woman of Zarephath and her son from starvation.[92] After the excitement and exhaustion of the confrontation on Mt. Carmel, it is Elijah who reassures King Ahab and gets him to eat and drink.[93] Subsequently, when Elijah comes to Elisha to anoint him as his successor, Elisha slaughters his two oxen to provide a feast for his friends and family to provide a feast for his family and friends to celebrate his elevation.[94] Finally, Elisha himself prescribes the simple cure of washing in the Jordan River seven times when the powerful Syrian general Naaman comes to him for a cure for his leprosy. "Go and wash seven times in the Jordan, and your skin will be restored and healed."[95] The story of Elijah teaches us that an intervention

90. 1 Kgs 19:4.
91. 1 Kgs 19:5–8.
92. 1 Kgs 17.
93. 1 Kgs 18:41–46.
94. 1 Kgs 19:19–21.
95. 2 Kgs 5:10.

to prevent suicide need not be grand—often simple is better—but it must be immediate.

The following four summary points stand out in these biblical narratives.

1. Life is ultimately hopeful, with an intrinsic sense of purpose. Heroic suicide and self-sacrifice are not necessary to provide meaning in life. Being human is enough.

2. Biblical figures, both men and women, are unable to develop a healthy view of themselves in society. People can and do change. They are able to be themselves within the context of relationships with others. They truly develop rather than cycle back and forth. When they reach a temporary dead end, help is available to help them restore their strength and move ahead.

3. Characters under attack are able to fight back and remain defiant. They do not have to convert an involuntary assault against them into the illusion that it is voluntary. When Rabbi Akiba is being tortured to death by the Romans for teaching the Hebrew Scriptures, he does not pretend he is dying willingly. Rather he shouts out the monotheistic prayer of his faith: "Hear oh Israel, the Lord our God, the Lord is One."

4. There is always an attempt to keep others from ending their lives (e.g., Elijah). This gesture does not have to be grand but often involves providing simple comforts such as food or drink and the opportunity to rest.

A Contemporary Illustration

Consider the following situation. You are standing in a subway station late at night, when somebody tries to jump to jump in front of an oncoming train right in front of you. What do you do next? This is exactly the theme of a 2011 HBO movie directed by Tommy Lee Jones entitled *The Sunset Limited*.[96] An adaptation of Cormac McCarthy's play, the movie takes place in a single room and consists of only two men, neither of whom are ever named, throughout its ninety-minute running time. It takes place in New York City and stars Jones and Samuel L. Jackson. Jackson plays a

96. Jones, *The Sunset Limited*.

black religious maintenance man who saves Jones's character, an alienated white college professor, from suicide. Jones (off-screen) has tried to jump in front of a subway train, the Sunset Limited, and Jackson has prevented him from jumping.

Jackson's character happened to be in an otherwise empty station when the train came through and saved Jones, who didn't want to be saved. But now the train is gone, and he reluctantly goes to Jackson's apartment, where the two fall into an intense conversation about what had just happened and why.

Locked in a philosophical debate, both passionately defend their personal credos and try to convert the other. Jones says that at a certain point there's no alternative to suicide. He's tired of living, he's got nothing more to live for, what's the point? Jackson's character doesn't exactly try to answer that question. Instead, he argues that there is a purpose behind everything God does and our job here is finding it. Jackson's own humble life suggests belief is most of what he has. But that is enough, he says, to keep him going. It kept him going through prison and keeps him getting by now as a maintenance man living in a threadbare tenement apartment.

The dialogue in this movie is brilliant, but this is the problem. It is all dialogue. Jackson's character, to be sure, tries to puncture the self-contained and destructive logic of the brilliant Jones-played professor. He tries, but he tries verbally. There is very little hands-on intervention of the type employed in the biblical story of Elijah described above. There does not seem to be much food in the apartment. Jackson attempts to give Jones coffee to drink, but nothing to eat, nor does he suggest Jones lay down to rest. Nor is there little, if any, physical contact. There is no discussion of any other part of their lives. Jackson does not probe to find out what are the passions of Jones's life. He does not engage Jones as to what things give Jones's life any meaning.

As the movie ends, Jones insists on leaving Jackson's apartment. Jones insists Jackson unbolt his door, and he leaves to what seems to be a very bleak fate. But Jackson's entire intervention attempt is undone by the fact that it remains on the rational, logical level that Jones surrounds himself with. This remains the Greek philosophical trap, which keeps the saving biblical message of being loved by a concerned Creator at such a remote level that it is not accessible.

Suppose while walking across a bridge in the late evening, you find a man perched on the edge ready to jump. When you approach him, he yells, "Leave me alone." What would you do? How would a psycho-biblical therapist handle a situation like this?

PSYCHO-BIBLICAL GUIDE NINE

Do not leave a distressed, demoralized, or suicidal person alone. Interventions need not be grand. Little actions such as a touch, a caress, food and drink, and a place to rest can help a person recover his strength and overcome a temporary melancholy, depression, or demoralization. It is important that you do not ignore a distressed person and leave him feeling isolated and rejected. It is important also that you seek help if you become distressed or suicidal. When the Greek warrior Ajax becomes suicidal, he is ignored, and given neither food nor drink nor companionship. He winds up killing himself. When the prophet Elijah expresses suicidal thoughts, he is given food and drink and a chance to rest and recovers his strength to go on to Horeb.

10

Relating to Misfortune

PSYCHO-BIBLICAL ISSUE TEN:

How should I interpret a misfortune or an unanticipated setback?
Should I interpret this as a sign of great meaning or attempt to delimit
its effects?

THE GREEK AND BIBLICAL views provide contrasting visions with regard to dealing with a misfortune. The Classical Greek view is deterministic, the essence of the tragic vision of man; the biblical view is hopeful and thus sees the possibility of change and transformation. The Greek view of tragedy can be contrasted with the biblical view of hope essential to therapy in three critical contrasts: the ability to overcome a dysfunctional family, the efficacy of prayer, and resiliency with regard to misfortune.

Consider the case of a dysfunctional family: the incestuous family of Oedipus. The Greek tragic vision is impossible to overcome. "But now, I am forsaken of the gods, son of a defiled mother, and successor to his bed who gave me my own wretched being."[1] However, a dysfunctional family background can be overcome in the biblical therapeutic vision: "Cast me not off, neither forsake me, O God of my salvation. For though my father and mother have forsaken me, the Lord will take me up."[2]

1. Sophocles, *Oedipus Rex*, lines 1359–61.
2. Ps 27:9–10.

For the Greeks, prayer is useless in this determined world: "Pray thou no more; for mortals have no escape from destined woe."[3] The biblical view, in contrast, believes in the profound efficacy of prayer, even in the most hopeless of situations: "Even if a sword's edge lies on the neck of a man he should not hold himself back from prayer.[4]"

The Greek mind, in the absence of a meaning-giving deity, seems to need to over-interpret or catastrophize a misfortune as a divine sign. The mature biblical mind, in contrast, need not do this. It is able to withstand all sorts of stressors because it is assured that it has been created by a loving God. Nowhere is this difference highlighted more than in the comparison of the stories of Zeno, founder of the Greek Stoic school of philosophy, and the biblical character of Job.

The Greek Narrative

According to the ancient Greek chronicler Diogenes Laertius, Zeno, founder of the Stoic school of philosophy, wrenched his toe on the way home from lecturing at the *stoa* (porch) and subsequently voluntarily held his breath until he died.[5] The description of Zeno's death is so implausible, indeed impossible, that it is worth commenting on. Breathing is the essence of life itself. Indeed the Scriptures portray life beginning with breathing. God breathes life into man. "Then the Lord God formed man of the dust of the ground, and breathed into his nostrils the breath of life; and man became a living soul."[6] For the living person, breathing is an involuntary act. If one tries to hold one's breath, he becomes faint or even unconscious, and begins to breathe again. So why then is Zeno described as "holding his breath until he dies?" Perhaps the meaning lies in Zeno's attempting to "play god," to try to make voluntary what is in actuality involuntary.

Furthermore, why should Zeno kill himself after so seemingly minor an annoyance as wrenching his toe? Understanding Zeno's actions necessitates examining more closely the Stoic view school of thought regarding suicide. Suicide must not be undertaken frivolously, "but if he (god) gives

3. Sophocles, *Antigone,* line 1336.

4. *b. Berachot* 10a.

5. Diogenes Laertius, *Lives,* 7.28.

6. Gen 2:7.

the signal to retreat as he did to Socrates, I must obey him who gives the signal, as I would a general."[7]

As the leader of the Stoic school, Zeno defined the goal of life as living in accordance with nature.[8] If this does not occur, suicide becomes the wise choice. The philosopher may choose his own mode of death just as he chooses a ship or a house. He leaves life as he would a banquet—when it is time.[9] Suicide must not be undertaken frivolously, but at the right time. But how does one know when the right time is? A person must look for a signal.

> Only let me not give up my heart faintheartedly or from some causal pretext. For again, God does not so desire; for he has no need of such a universe and of such men who go to and fro upon earth. But if he (god) gives the signal to retreat as he did to Socrates, I must obey him who gives the signal, as I would a general.[10]

This then becomes the key issue for Zeno and the Stoics. They await a signal that it is time to depart this life. In this quote, the contemporary writers Droge and Tabor[11] find a precedent for "rational suicide." Suicide is condoned when it is necessary and rational; it is condemned when it is irrational. A rational suicide is preceded by an apparently divine signal that the time to die is at hand. An irrational suicide is not preceded by such a signal. In other words, Zeno killed himself by holding his breath, not because he stubbed his toe, nor because he was in pain, nor even because he was depressed, but because he bought into the notion that the event of stubbing his toe represented a divine signal to depart.[12]

It turns out that the tendency to find cosmic significance in a minor misfortune (i.e., we will call this tendency "zenoism") is destructive for Zeno in that it leads to his suicide. At the same time, however, this coping strategy may provide him with a *meaning structure* that is otherwise missing in his life. In a certain sense, it provides a sense of the heroic—Zeno is important enough to be called by the gods to depart. Although zenoism may involve a tendency to over-interpret an objectively innocuous event,

7. Epictetus, *Discourses*, 1.29.

8. Diogenes Laertius, *Lives*, 7.87.

9. Seneca, *Letters from a Stoic*, 70.11; Plotinus, *On Suicide*, 1.9.

10. Epictetus, *Discourses*, 1.29.

11. Droge and Tabor, *A Noble Death*, 29–39.

12. Ibid., 31.

it still provides an antidote to a basic meaninglessness in his life. Remember, prayer is useless in this determined world.

If we may psychologize for a moment, it is not much of a stretch to see Zeno as preoccupied with his aging. Despite his popularity, Zeno may feel increasingly alone. He seems to jump at the chance to insert meaning into his life through interpreting cosmic significance to his relatively minor misfortune. Interpreting his rather innocuous mishap as a divine signal to depart in effect provides him with permission to commit suicide.[13] In this sense, his suicide is *rationalized* rather than *rational*, masking the underlying psychodynamic issues of gerophobia and loss of control.

It may well be that the tendency to find cosmic significance in a minor misfortune, as destructive as it proves for an aging Zeno, may represent a coping strategy, which provides him with a heroic meaning structure that is otherwise missing in his life. Zeno feels important enough to be called by the gods to depart. It perhaps makes him fell less alone.

Four events stand out in this narrative.

1. The aging Zeno stubs his toe on the way home from giving a lecture on his philosophy.

2. There is no sign that this represents a major catastrophe, yet he interprets this as a sign from the gods he should depart.

3. This belief, though exaggerated and obviously self-destructive, provides him with a sense of meaning.

4. He holds his breath until he dies. This act has been seen as a prototype of "rational suicide."

The Biblical Narrative

The biblical figure of Job is very different. God's adversary Satan tests Job by assaulting him, with God's permission, with many crushing misfortunes.[14] First, Job is struck by the death of his servants, the loss of his livestock, and then, terribly, the deaths of all of his children (unnamed). Yet he reaffirms his faith in God: "Naked came I out of my mother's womb, and naked shall I return thither; the Lord gave, and the Lord hath taken

13. Plato, *Phaedo*, 62b-c; Cicero, *De Finibus*, 3.60–61.

14. In a monotheistic Jewish interpretation, Satan is not an independent figure but is subordinate to God himself. He is acting more like a prosecutor than anything else.

away; blessed be the name of the Lord."[15] Then, he is afflicted with severe skin inflammations all over his body. And finally, his wife urges him to blaspheme God and die. Job rejects his wife's view: "What? shall we receive good at the hand of God, and shall we not receive evil?"[16] Though he is deeply grieved, he reaffirms his relationship with his Creator. "Though He slay me, yet will I trust in Him; but I will argue my ways before Him."[17]

Though he is obviously deeply stressed and distressed, Job is portrayed as rejecting suicide and despair. He seems to have an intrinsic sense of life's meaning, which provides a prophylactic against over-interpreting events that happen to him in a suicidal manner. Indeed he rejects his friends' interpretation that his misfortunes are due to his actions. In this regard he eventually confronts God himself who answers him out of the whirlwind and tells him that God's ways are beyond human understanding.[18]

This is a very interesting response with double-edged implications. On the one hand God's response represents a strong rebuke to the friends of Job, who continually accuse Job of guilty behavior leading to his afflictions. On the other hand God is rebuking Job himself for demanding tit-for-tat accountability. In other words, his afflictions are no indicator that he has sinned, nor does his just and righteous behavior ensure that he won't suffer afflictions. These of course are the two polarities of a simple-minded "just world hypothesis," in which the world is a just and orderly place where people always get what they deserve.[19] If one suffers, one deserves it. Rather, God is communicating that God's ways are beyond human understanding.

Only when Job accepts this conception does he become restored, two-fold, in everything. God, in fact, asks Job to pray for his doubting friends, which he does, and Job names his first daughter Yemima (Jemimah), meaning dove and deriving from the Hebrew word *yom* meaning "day."[20] The name Yemima has also been interpreted as meaning "day bright" or "being beautiful like the sun of the day" because Job has now

15. Job 1:13–21.
16. Job 2:7–10.
17. Job 13:15.
18. Job 38–41.
19. Lerner, *Just World Hypothesis,* 1030–51.
20. Job 42:1–17.

emerged from the "night of his affliction."[21] Job in fact gives all three of his new daughters names (the second being Keziah and the third being Kerenhappuch) in distinction to the lack of names provided for his original three daughters who died at the beginning of the book. Perhaps this is an indicant that Job recognizes each of his new daughters unique personalities more than he had his original daughters.[22]

In contrast to Zeno, Job does not need to milk his situation for meaning. Job is already in a relationship with a Creator who gives his life intrinsic meaning. Job's meaning is to live—and to overcome his misfortunes. In the biblical framework, Job sees that God gives and takes away life, but this is not the same as searching for a divine signal that it is time to depart. Therefore, Job is not goaded to see his far greater misfortunes as a sign to exit this world, but rather as a test of his faith.

We should remember that Zeno kills himself not because he broke his toe *per se*, but because he interpreted this event as a divine signal to depart.[23] Job, in contrast, does not need this interpretive structure, as he knows he is in a relationship with a Creator who gives his life intrinsic meaning. Job's meaning is to live and overcome his misfortunes. Thus he does not need to over-interpret a misfortune in order to find meaning. Rather, secure in his sense that he has been created by a loving God, Job is able to delimit the effects of a misfortune and not give up hope. He manifests a sense of resiliency created by a sense of secure parenting and the ability to hope. The Jewish view believes in the efficacy of prayer, even in the most hopeless of situations: "Even if a sword's edge lies on the neck of a man he should not hold himself back from prayer."[24]

Job's travails and recovery can be highlighted by the following four events.

1. Job is assailed by grievous afflictions, first losing his wealth, his children, and finally his health.

2. Despite the criticism and blaming of his friends, Job refuses to accept that he deserves his lot.

21. One can see this astounding recovery in our own times, with all the "Yemimas," male and female, dancing and singing in sun-kissed and bright modern Israel, their parents having emerged from the night of the Nazi holocaust *(shoa)* in grey and dismal Europe.

22. Job 1:13–19.

23. Droge, and Tabor, *A Noble Death*, 31.

24. *b. Berachot* 10a.

3. He even rejects his wife's despair and reaffirms his sense of his relationship with his Creator. He reaffirms life.

4. He encounters God's explanation that his covenant is beyond Job's understanding. When he accepts this, all is restored to him.

Two Contemporary Illustrations

Let's consider two contemporary illustrations. The first involved the death of one Martha Wichorek, Case #70 of the physician-assisted suicides performed by the late Jack Kevorkian. As I was psychological consultant and director of the *Detroit Free Press*–Wayne State University Study of Physician Assisted Suicide, I was a public figure in Detroit regarding these cases in the early 1990s. I thus found myself the recipient of a series of letters Martha sent publicly to a number of officials and professionals, in which she advocated for a state euthanasia clinic.[25] Below is an excerpt from an early letter written and sent by this highly functioning woman:

> When "life" (being able to do things for yourself and others) is taken away, unless a heart attack or accident strikes first, every human being usually descends into the "miserable existence" stage (cannot do anything for yourself or others—totally helpless). This stage of that life-death cycle can last weeks, months or years and is the most dreaded of human experiences.[26]

Martha went on for three full pages speaking about the suffering of those in the "miserable existence stage," which she also called the "other death row." Among the indignities of the "miserable existence stage," she included (1) nursing home or hospital tests and procedures, (2) living with children, (3) hospice, (4) in-home and visiting nurse arrangements, (5) living wills, and (6) committing suicide without the help of a doctor. She called for a state-approved euthanasia clinic, and she signed the letter, "A still clear thinking 81-year-old human being." Since I was concerned about Martha, I called her as soon as I received this letter. My conversation with her revealed that Martha had lost her husband to cancer three years previously, and that she had three grown daughters. She lived alone and, aside from some normal ailments associated with aging, was in reasonably good

25. Kaplan and Leonhardi, "Kevorkian," 267–70.
26. Wichorek, letter to author, 2 December 1996.

health. She was not terminal nor in acute physical pain. In fact, she seemed to be active in her community and had a very sharp mind.

In April 1997, many of us again received letters from Martha, this time from a hospital where she had undergone a hysterectomy after episodes of vaginal bleeding. She indicated was doing fine and acknowledged that "she was getting stronger," but she described the "torture" she was enduring, specifying the following: (1) "IVs with anesthetics, nutrients, etc."; (2) "tight rubber stockings that stretched from my toes to the crotch, and expanding and contracting legging attached to a motor for better blood circulation"; (3) "tubes in my nose, for oxygen"; (4) "breathing tubes to exercise my lungs"; (5) "blood pressure and temperature checks every hour, an EKG, blood drawn for lab tests, etc."; and (6) "I was expected to walk, one day after surgery, alone from the bathroom, holding onto the IV pole."

All of us who have undergone surgery recognize these "tortures" as unpleasant but temporary and quite bearable, and recognize that they are not tortures at all but simply minor annoyances that are necessary to facilitate a quick and complete recovery. Martha's comments indicate that she also recognized the reason these measures were undertaken; yet she seemed to regard each of these measures as an assault to her dignity that made "life not worth living." Martha spent only three days in the hospital and recovered quite quickly from her surgery.

Yet it was scarcely eight months later, on December 3, 1997, that Martha Wichorek became the seventieth documented physician-assisted suicide conducted by Jack Kevorkian and his associates. The physical autopsy revealed no anatomical evidence of any disease, indicating that her sense of hopelessness had little to do with her physical condition.

It is evident that Martha, like Zeno, catastrophized her event, and saw in it a reason to die. She definitely was following a Greek pattern of over-interpreting a minor misfortune, perhaps to provide her otherwise empty life with a purpose (euthanasia or physician-assisted suicide), as lethal as that proved to be to her.

The life and death of the late Joseph Cardinal Bernardin of Chicago presents a clear biblical contrast with regard to dealing with a misfortune. At sixty-eight, Bernardin received a diagnosis of terminal pancreatic cancer. He refused prolonged treatment, and said he found peace "by putting himself in God's hands." But he did not hasten his death or fight for a control of his death, as did Martha Wichorek. Bernardin lived his life as fully as his strength allowed to the very end, completing many final tasks. Even more, Bernardin turned his dying process into one of his most profound teaching moments, living life with dignity and gracefulness till he was taken away. He did not need to catastrophize his situation, but indeed coped with the discomfort he was surely in, and lived his life as fully as he could till the end. He finished a book on interfaith relations, saw friends and family for the last time, and wrote final letters and Chanukah and Christmas cards before he died. He did not try to milk his death for meaning missing in his life, but accepted it as a natural part of the human condition.

A beautiful piece by Martha Holstein describes most poetically the way Cardinal Bernardin died.

> Because he was so public in his dying, Bernardin opened a moral space that encourages us to reflect about the preconditions for a good death. With all the attention now focused on physician-assisted suicide, we easily forget that most people do not ask their physicians for assistance in dying. Rather they want help in dying well, relatively free of pain and suffering, and with their dignity intact . . .
>
> We can never eliminate all suffering. Nor can those who see suffering as ennobling ask others, who may not share this view, to suffer as exemplars for the rest of us. Yet, we can hope to have some of the blessings that made it possible for Bernardin to die as he did. Bernardin's death also asks us to attend to how we live—to be open to giving and receiving love, and to understand that the choices we make affect not only our life but also our death. Thinking about the meaning of our lives is not a task for its last moment. The cardinal nurtured in us the courage to think about a good death for ourselves and those we love, and for holding out the hope that dying well is truly possible.[27]

Note how different Bernardin's stance in this regard is from Martha Wichorek's. He did not catastrophize minor discomforts but, like Job, accepted some pain and suffering. And furthermore, he did not focus solely on death, as do Zeno and the other Stoics, but on his whole life.

> The cardinal's death thus taught that living and dying are parts of a whole. Some years ago, upon the sudden death of a close friend, the emergency room physician said to me, "Remember what the Orthodox Jews say, live each day as if it were your last . . . "[28]

27. Holstein, "Bernardin's Way," 1.

28. Ibid.

PSYCHO-BIBLICAL GUIDE TEN

Do not exaggerate the import of a particular negative event. To do
this is destructive, and you should consider changing your approach.
A single misfortune or setback can be seen as just that. A setback does
not indicate that you are not of intrinsic worth. Do not catastrophize
or give up hope. Zeno the Stoic kills himself after stubbing his toe. He
catastrophizes the significance of a relatively minor event in an attempt
to find meaning in his life. Job does not need to do this as he has an
intrinsic sense of worth and meaning. To the extent you find intrinsic
meaning in your life, this will obviate the need to catastrophize.

Conclusion

THIS BOOK HAS EXAMINED Greek narratives and attempted to show their detrimental effect on modern psychology as played out in ten contemporary life issues: 1) Relating to the Environment, 2) Relating to Another as Yourself, 3) Relating to Authority, 4) Relating to the Opposite Sex, 5) Relating to a Son, 6) Relating to a Daughter, 7) Relating to Siblings, 8) Relating Body to Soul, 9) Relating to a Self-Destructive Person, and 10) Relating to Misfortune. In each case, the Greek narratives leave people trapped, or worse. It is impossible to escape one's fate, no matter how hard one tries, and death is often seen as the only escape. For each of these ten issues, we have suggested contrasting biblical narratives and visions. People are not trapped, change is possible, and life is of intrinsic value.

Why then have many of our poets and writers simplistically idealized Greek and Roman civilizations? For example, Edgar Allen Poe, in his poem *To Helen,* writes "to the glory that was Greece and the grandeur that was Rome."[1] Phillip Slater forces us to address the reality: "When the well-known classicist Gilbert Murray tells us that 'Greek thought, always sincere and daring, was seldom brutal, seldom ruthless or cruel . . . ,' he is asking us to share a vision which is not only false but emasculated and bloodless. To recreate Greece in the image of Plato is to reduce a rich and vibrant society to its most arteriosclerotic by-product."[2]

One fundamental difference between biblical and Greek narratives is the way they portray the receipt of information from an authority. In the Greek narrative of Oedipus, Oedipus is living in Corinth with his adopted father King Polybus and his adopted mother, the Dorian Merope. After hearing a chance comment questioning his identity, Oedipus goes to Delphi to consult the Oracle. The Oracle informs Oedipus that he is destined to kill his father and marry his mother, but neglects to tell him

---

1. Poe, "To Helen."
2. Slater, *Glory of Hera,* xxii–xxiii.

that he is living with his adopted father and mother.[3] To avoid this fate *(moira* in Greek*)*, Oedipus leaves Corinth and returns to Thebes, where unbeknownst to him, his biological father and mother live, and we have described at length the sad result. A reasonable person must ask, if the Oracle at Delphi really had Oedipus's interests at heart, why she did not conclude her warning with the critical information that Oedipus was safe from his fate as long as he stayed in Corinth and did not return to Thebes? In this sense, the Oracle can be said to be passively lying through the withholding of critical information. What it neglected to say provoked the tragedy of Oedipus.

The biblical paradigm regarding receipt of information is very different. The God of Scriptures warns Adam not to eat of the fruit of the tree of knowledge of good and evil lest he surely die.[4] What is left unsaid is that although eating of the forbidden fruit will cause Adam and his wife to be exiled from Eden and lose personal immortality, it will open up their eyes as to sexual knowledge, allowing the fulfilment of God's command "to be fruitful and multiply."[5] However, this is not really a passive lie as in the Greek account, nor does it lead to anything destructive to humankind. Although Adam and his wife lose their personal immortality, they become parents and thus participate in cross-generational continuity. Indeed after they are banished from Eden, Adam names his wife Eve *(Chava* in Hebrew*)* because she will be the mother of all the living.[6]

Another key difference between Greek and biblical conceptions of society and life can be seen in the different strata from which they see the world created. As we mentioned in chapter 1, the Greek world begins in *chaos,* while the Hebrew world begins in *formlessness (tohu vovohu).* Although many writers seem to have equated these two concepts, they seem to us to be fundamentally different. The first (chaos) implies dangerous upheaval, which must be controlled and even subdued. The second (formlessness) does not imply this upheaval, but simply a nonform, which requires shape and definition but need not be subdued or conquered. As such, the Greek world seems to dread the future and fear it while the biblical world embraces it and dares to hope.

3. Sophocles, *Oedipus Rex,* lines 776–93.

4. Gen 2:15–18.

5. Gen 1:28.

6. Gen 3:17–21.

Order in the Greek political world is stasis or control (always in an uneasy battle with chaos). Change is a threat to this equilibrium and this is why Plato elevates the "eternal" being over the "transitory" becoming. In the biblical world, life has a purpose and constructive change is embraced, not feared. The glue of the biblical world is the Creator. Thus, change is not threatening and the future need not be dreaded.

Nothing illustrates this difference better than a comparison of Greek and biblical narratives regarding incestuous relations. The Greek story of Oedipus has been discussed previously in this book and is well known. It is powerfully described in Sophocles' monumental play *Oedipus Rex*. Oedipus unknowingly kills his biological father, Laius, and equally unknowingly marries his mother, Jocasta, becomes King of Thebes, and engages in incestuous relations with his mother. Out of this union, four children emerge: two sons, Eteocles and Polyneices, and two daughters, Antigone and Ismene. Oedipus's behavior as king seems exemplary. He seems concerned for his subjects, trying to end a great plague that has fallen upon Thebes. Oedipus's brother-in-law, Creon, tells him that the god has sent the plague due to a "defiling thing, which hath been harbored in this land . . . " Oedipus innocently and conscientiously asks how Thebes can be cleansed. Creon responds, "By banishing a man, or by bloodshed in quittance of bloodshed, since it is that blood which brings the tempest on our city."[7]

When Oedipus, acting out of noble impulses, discovers his identity, he is filled with shame and self-loathing:

> So had I not come to shed my father's blood, not been called among men the spouse of her from whom I sprang; but now am I forsaken of the gods, son of a defiled mother, successor to his bed who gave me mine own wretched being; and if there be yet a woe surpassing woes, it hath become the portion of Oedipus.[8]

The Greek mindset here seems not to be concerned with the righteousness or lack of righteousness of Oedipus's act (after all, it was a case of mistaken identity) but rather is obsessed with the idea that Oedipus's incest with his mother has "polluted" the city of Thebes.

As the narrative proceeds, Oedipus rushes to kill Jocasta:

---

7. Sophocles, *Oedipus Rex*, lines 98–99, 101–2.
8. Ibid., 1348–52.

> To and fro he went, asking us to give him a sword,—asking where
> he should find the wife who was no wife, but a mother whose
> womb had borne alike himself and his children.[9]

Oedipus, seeing that his mother has hung herself, plunges the golden brooches on her dress into his eyes, as he does not want to face his biological parents in the next world.[10]

More tragic events unfold consequentially. Aeschylus described it thusly in *The Seven against Thebes*: The blinded Oedipus wanders miserable and alone. Feeling mistreated and abandoned by his two sons, he curses them to kill one another.

> A curse prophetic and bitter (of Oedipus on his sons)—The glory
> of wealth and pride, with iron, not gold, in your hand ye shall
> come, at the last to divide.[11]

One brother, Eteocles, becomes king of Thebes and exiles his brother Polyneices, a rival for the kingship. Polyneices enlists the aid of Argos and leads an army against Thebes to seize the throne. The two brothers do slay each other at the seventh gate of Thebes, fulfilling the curse of Oedipus.

> And both alike, even now and here have closed their suit, with
> steel for arbiter. And lo, the fury-fiend of Oedipus, their sire, hath
> brought his curse to consummation dire. Each in the left side smitten, see them laid—the children of one womb, slain by a mutual
> doom![12]

This story continues in Sophocles' *Antigone*. Creon, who has now assumed the vacant throne of Thebes, issues a proclamation that the body of Eteocles, the defender of Thebes, be given the full funeral honors due a hero, while the corpse of Polyneices, the attacker, be left unburied, without proper funeral rites, a punishment and a slight the Greeks viewed with horror. Their sister Antigone refuses to follow Creon's order and attempts to bury her brother. Creon responds by ordering her buried alive. Antigone subsequently hangs herself while in the vault below.

But we are not finished yet. After finding her hanging, Antigone's suitor, Haemon falls on his sword after unsuccessfully trying to kill his

---

9. Ibid., 1256.

10. Ibid., 1261–74, 1373–77.

11. Aeschylus, *Seven Against Thebes*, lines 785–86.

12. Ibid., 879–924.

father Creon. Upon learning of her son's death, Haemon's mother Eurydice stabs herself with a "keen knife."[13]

One must ask, Why does all this happen? Where is the stopper in Greek thinking? Why couldn't the family of Oedipus and Jocasta, though based mistakenly on incest, live happily, or at least reasonably? What is illuminating here is the etymological derivation of the name *Antigone* itself. *Anti* means "against' or "opposite to," and *gone* has been interpreted as denoting "birth or offspring," or "mother," as one who gives birth. In this view, Antigone denotes "opposed to motherhood." A related derivation sees her name denoting "anti-generative," or even "anti-male" from *gony* meaning "seed or semen," or even "anti-ancestor" from *gon.* A less popular derivation views *gon* as denoting "bend," thus interpreting Antigone as denoting "unbending."

In all these derivations, Antigone is either against the past, the present, or the future, and a far cry from biblical woman Eve both as *Chava,* "mother of all living," and as *ezer kenegdo,* "helpmeet opposite." Antigone thus can be seen as standing in opposition to the Jewish conception of *mi dor la dor,* "from generation to generation," and in this sense as standing against the biblical idea of history itself.

The biblical world too has several significant incest stories; yet they have far more positive outcomes. Consider first the incest between Lot and his daughters. After the destruction of Sodom in which their fiancés have been killed, the two daughters of Lot get their father drunk and lie with him because they believe he is the last man left in the world. "And the first-born said unto the younger: 'Our father is old, and there is not a man in the earth to come in unto us after the manner of all the earth. Come let us make our father drink wine, and we will lie with him, that we may preserve the seed of our father . . . '"[14] Both daughters conceive, and two boys are born, the son of the elder daughter named Moab, deriving from the Hebrew words *Mo-Ab,* "from the father," the ancestor of the Moabites.

Among the Moabites is Ruth who marries an Israelite. After her husband's death, Ruth chooses to remain with her mother-in-law, Naomi, and joins the Israelite nation. In a very moving speech, Ruth says to Naomi, "Whither thou goest, I will go; whither thou lodgest, I will lodge; thy

---

13. Sophocles, *Antigone,* lines 406–18, 891–96, 1223–36, 1293–1302.

14. Gen 19:31.

people shall be my people and thy God my God."[15] The incestuous nature of the origin of Ruth's family is never mentioned, and subsequently, Ruth marries Boaz,[16] and through their union, Ruth bears Obed, and becomes the ancestress of King David.[17] And in the Christian tradition the ancestress of Jesus of Nazareth.[18]

A second biblical incest story also has a positive outcome—that of the sexual encounter between Judah and his daughter-in-law Tamar. Judah, Jacob's fourth son, is a leader among his brethren, indeed the royal family of David and Solomon will stem from him. In Genesis 38, Judah separates himself from the society of his brothers and goes into business with Hirah the Adulamite, a local merchant. He marries a local woman, the daughter of Shua the Canaanite (that is, someone outside the family) and the couple eventually raise a family of three sons. Er, the eldest, marries; but God slays Er for an unspecified wickedness, and his widow Tamar is left with no children.

The Hebrew levirate law required that the brother (or close relative) of the deceased marry his childless widow to try to have a son with her—a son who would be an heir to the deceased. So Judah instructs Onan, his second son, to take this responsibility with Tamar. But Onan does not want to "give seed to his brother"; pretending to consummate his legitimate (but unwanted) marriage to Tamar, he allows his seed to fall to the ground rather than produce a son to carry on his brother Er's heritage (thus the term *onanism*). Onan's behavior is also displeasing to God, and like his older brother, he also dies. Judah then tells Tamar to return to her father's house and live life as a widow while she waits for his third son, Shelah, to reach the age when he will be able to marry her and fulfill the levirate requirement. But in point of fact, Judah, seeing that his two older sons have married Tamar and died shortly after, fears that he will be sending Shelah to the same fate. Time passes, and Tamar, who is no fool,

---

15. Ruth 1:16.

16. Ruth 4:13. Israelites are forbidden to marry Moabites and Ammonites not because of the incestuous origin of the people, but because their men did not show hospitality to the Israelites in the Sinai and also because "they hired Balaam son of Beor from Pethor in Aram Naharaim to curse you" (Deut 23:4). The Talmud expresses the view that the prohibition only applied to male Moabites, who were not allowed to marry Jews (*y. Yevamot* 8:3). Female Moabites, when converted to Judaism, were permitted to marry with only the normal prohibition of a convert marrying a *kohen* (high priest) applying.

17. Ruth 4:17.

18. Matt 1:1–17.

realizes that Judah does not intend to send his third son to marry her, but she is determined to bear children for Er's sake as well as to accept and participate in the God-given mission of Jacob's family.[19]

In the meantime, Judah's wife dies. After his period of mourning, the new widower Judah goes to Timnah with his friend and business associate Hirah for the annual shearing of the sheep, an important event that is celebrated with feasting and drinking. Tamar hears of this and is determined to practice a deception of her own, a lie the purpose of which is honorable and will be, in Scripture's terms, "eye-opening." Dressed as a prostitute and with her face covered, Tamar approaches Judah at a crossroads as he is returning from the shearing. Though it is proscribed by everything in his upbringing, Judah decides to have relations with this "prostitute" and begins to negotiate a price.[20] We should note that Tamar, in her deception of her father-in-law, is sitting at a *petach anayim*, which is generally translated as "crossroads"; but the Hebrew term, taken literally, would mean "opening of the eyes."

By deceiving Judah, Tamar opens his eyes and reveals to Judah what was best in him. When Tamar is threatened with death for adultery, Judah assumes responsibility for his act and says, "She was righteous (because I did not give her to Shelah). It is by me."[21] In impregnating Tamar and acknowledging the act, Judah himself will thus beget twin sons, Perez and Zerah, to replace the dead Er and Onan. Perez will become an ancestor of Boaz and of King David and his dynasty.

Both the above Greek and biblical narratives stories relate an act of incest.[22] Yet the story of Oedipus and his mother ends in disaster while that of Lot and his daughters and of Judah and his daughter-in-law Tamar end happily. Why? The real difference lies in the different reasons for the incest as a reflection of the underlying attitude towards the future and how that impacts on society. The very beginning of the Oedipus legend reflects the Greek fear of the future illustrated in the etymology, presented above, of the name Antigone. It portrays Laius as hearing from an oracle that his newborn son will kill him and marry his wife, the child's mother, should he "reach man's estate." Oedipus is seen as a threat to displace his

19. Gen 38:1–11.

20. Gen 38:12–19.

21. Gen 38:25–27.

22. Tamar's liaison with her father-in-law was to be forbidden in later biblical law; but at this time it was a legitimate form of Levirate Marriage.

father Laius, and thus must be destroyed. The father, afraid of the future, has the power of infant exposure and uses it. This is the act that precipitates the later incest, unaware as Laius may be, and the entire tragic events of the house of Oedipus.

This view is foreign and incomprehensible to a biblical view of society. Why doesn't Laius glory in the arrival of a new son who hopefully will surpass him? He is a link in the chain between generations (*mi dor la dor*). In the biblical view, the father is not the owner of his son as with the Roman *patria potestas,* nor does he hold the power of infant exposure. The Bible sees the relationship between father and son in terms of the fulfillment of the covenant. Indeed, this is what the ceremony of the covenant of circumcision (*b'rit ha milah*) represents. Any urge of a father to destroy his son is superseded by the command to the father to teach his children thoroughly.[23] The father's identity is not threatened by the son; he wants to see his son develop and surpass him.

The incest stories of Lot and of Judah reflect this biblical hope in the future. Lot's daughters make their father drunk and lie with him because they think he is the last man left in the world. Tamar plays a prostitute with her widowed father-in-law Judah to carry on the tribe of Judah. These women do not fear the future, but embrace it.

No biblical story illustrates a faith in the future more than Miriam's calling on her parents to remarry to have more children, even in the face of Pharaoh's decree to murder all the newborn boys of the Israelites. The Babylonian Talmud fills out the rather cryptic account in Exodus 1–2 by telling how, when Pharaoh decrees that all Israelite infant boys be killed, Amram and Jochebed separate in despair over the doom that would fall on any male child they would bear. Miriam, still a very little girl, goes to her father and argues: "Pharaoh's decree affects only the sons; your act affects daughters as well." Amram accepts his daughter's advice and her sense of faith, and he and Jochebed remarry (Miriam actually dances at their wedding). In due course, this reunion produces Moses.[24]

This is the difference between these Greek and biblical "incest" stories, and it is reflective of the underlying stance toward the future in Greek and biblical thinking. Beneath it all, Greek society fears change

23. Deut. 6:7; *b. Kiddushin* 30a.
24. *b. Sotah* 12b.

and the future. This may be why Plato elevates "being" over "becoming."[25] The goal of the Greek political world is control over underlying chaos and ultimately change itself which is seen as a threat to a static equilibrium and order. The biblical view in contrast embraces the reality that life inherently is not static, and that things change over time.[26] Such change need not be chaotic but can be purposive. Life cannot simply be described by a static logical syllogism.

For Greeks and Indo-Europeans, space is fundamental to time; in fact, in an Indo-European model time is basically spatial, namely, as a series of points that follow one another in a line, past (behind us), present and future (before us). For the Hebrew way of thinking, however, time is fundamental, not space. The Hebrew language has essentially two tenses, corresponding to the completeness or incompleteness of the events that make up time. Hebrew tenses refer to events: those which has been concluded and those which has not been concluded, or roughly the equivalent of the perfect and the imperfect tenses. Consider the simple western syllogism: All B is C, all A is B, therefore all A is C. While logically correct in a narrow sense, it is psychologically limiting from a biblical point of view. Because in reality, all B may be C at Time 1 but not at Time 2 and so on. In other words, the statement may be imperfect rather than perfect.

Consider the following example in the Exodus narrative. One might argue that 1) "No one with a slave mentality is fit to enter "The Promised Land" 2) The Israelites fleeing Egypt have this slave mentality. Therefore 3) They are not fit to enter the promised land." What is squeezed out of this syllogism is the biblical sense of time as process and the basic idea that people can change. Thus 4) the Israelites might not be ready to enter the Promised Land at Time 1, -only Caleb and Joshua of the 12 spies seem ready,[27] but forty years later at Time 2 they are ready to do so under the leadership of Joshua.[28]

The glue of the biblical world is the Creator. Thus, change is not threatening, and the future need not be dreaded. The constructive use of time enables the progression from victim to a survivor to thriver.

25. Plato, *Symposium.*

26. Boman, *Hebrew Thought*; Bergson, *Time and Free Will*

27. Num 13–14.

28. Josh 3:1–5:12.

No doubt Freud observed the father-son struggle among his patients in Vienna and recognized this complex in the myths of ancient Greece and even that a father-son conflict deterministically emerges out of the Olympian theogony itself. Yet the question emerges as to why Freud, a Jew, even if in his own terms a "godless Jew," so ignored his own Hebrew tradition at the expense of those of classical Greece. In the introduction, we produced a letter from Freud indicating his unwillingness to even consider that his own biblical and Jewish tradition might provide a more complete resolution of the Oedipal conflict than he himself offers.

In *The Future of an Illusion*, Freud states his view of "religious doctrines as illusions"[29] and religion as "the universal obsessional neurosis of humanity; arising out of the Oedipus complex."[30] Yet Freud's fascination with the Oedipus Complex seems to ignore the fact that it emerges out of the Olympian creation story or theogony, itself a tale of the genesis of the Greek pantheon of gods and absolutely a religious system, though not a monotheistic one.

Why was Freud so dismissive of his biblical tradition? One answer is that Freud was committed to the German value of *Bildung*, which reflected the post-enlightenment, neo-humanist pedagogical tradition that became the intellectual home of German scholars and the surest route for aspiring Jewish academics to achieve social respectability and professional advancement. The cosmopolitan, ardently secular ethos of *Bildung* tilted Freud towards narratives emerging from classical Greece and made it difficult, if not impossible, for Freud to interpret the Bible favorably.

This is especially unfortunate in light of Erich Wellisch's eloquent argument presented in chapter 5 that the Akedah Motif between Abraham and Isaac provides a different resolution for father-son conflict and a different basis for the superego than that provided in the Freud's treatment of the Oedipus Complex. For Wellisch, this Akedah resolution is based more on mutual love and a sense of continuity between father and son than one based on a sense of fear. We have argued the important role of covenantal circumcision (*b'rit ha-milah*) in this regard: the son knows the father could have castrated him, but didn't, penile circumcision the physical representation of the father assenting to his son becoming his successor. Indeed the resolution of the Akedah narrative in chapter 5 occurs when, as Abraham is

29. Freud, *Future of an Illusion*, 43.
30. Ibid., 55.

poised to slaughter Isaac, the angel sent by God stays Abraham's hand with the famous words: "Lay not thine hand upon the lad."[31]

This is usually interpreted as a biblical prohibition against child sacrifice, once and for all. More than that, it sets the stage for a covenant of love between father and son, with the possibility of a superego based on love rather than on fear. The son gains a teacher, and the father an heir, and they have a joint vested interest in a good father-son relationship. Indeed this view is reflected in the words of the prophet Malachi (also cited earlier):

> . . . And He shall turn the heart of the fathers to the children,
> And the heart of the children to their fathers . . . [32]

Yet Freud appears resistant to this line of thinking and remains immersed within the cyclical Greek mindset so pervasive in the Europe of his time. In his monumental philosophical work *Athens and Jerusalem*,[33] Lev Shestov argues that European man has been basically Greek rather than Hebrew. European man has shied away from the biblical proclamation that God created the heaven and the earth, instead sub-ordering him to the very natural and material laws. For Shestov, the Creator of the world has himself become subordinate to necessity, which he created and which, without at all seeking or discovering, has become the sovereign of the universe.

Freud is one of Shestov's "European men" and, as such, seems not even willing to consider Shestov's radical conception that God created nature and is thus able to change what seem to be immutable natural laws (for example, the immutable conflict between father and son foretold by Earth and Sky). Max Eitingon, a friend of Shestov, sent Freud one of Shestov's books. Freud's reply gives ample evidence as to his resistance to and limitations in understanding biblical and Hebrew thinking. "You cannot imagine how unaffected I am by these convoluted philosophical discussions."[34]

Freud thus remains trapped within the cyclical Greek mindset and is left without the counter-narrative that biblical psychology provides.

31. Gen 22: 9–12.

32. Mal 3:24.

33. Shestov, *Athens and Jerusalem*.

34. Rolnik, *Freud in Zion*, 56. Thanks are once again due to Daniel Algom for providing the translation of the Hebrew passage.

Freud tries his best to bring the unconscious father-son conflict to conscious awareness in order to make it amenable to control. Yet he has no real way of transforming it in the way that Erich Wellisch has called for. Yosef Yerushalmi puts it this way: "Like Sisyphus pushing his rock, Oedipus and Laius must contend forever. At one point in the cycle, the father must be slain by the son; at another, the return of the repressed, the father returns; the return is only illusion, for the cycle will begin again."[35]

Freud's lack of a counter-narrative leaves him unable to offer his patients any real sense of hope in a happier life, which a biblical psychology may provide, but offers just an amelioration of an unhappy one. That Freud seems be aware of the limitations of psychoanalysis in this regard is reflected in his often-quoted statement at the end of his essay on the psychotherapy of hysteria. In response to a question from a patient as to how psychoanalysis will help him, Freud responds: "I do not doubt that it would be easier for fate to take away your suffering than it would for me. But you will see for yourself that much has been gained if we succeed in turning your hysterical misery into common unhappiness. Having restored your inner life, you will be better able to arm yourself against that unhappiness."[36]

This is hardly a positive worldview. However, our group of biblical psychologists are "American men and women," not "European men and women," and as such we are less trapped by the Greek mindset described by Shestov. As Americans, we are more biblically open than our European counterparts and thus are open to an alternate, more hopeful vision. We are hopeful that the ten guides presented in this book will provide a blueprint for the reader and for all people interested in living a fuller and more meaningful life.

Nicholas Wolterstorff, the Noah Porter Professor Emeritus of Philosophical Theology at Yale University, puts it this way:

> The ancient Greek writers had a tragic view of life. Theirs was a culture of honor and shame; they admired the hero . . . [However] the biblical God is not one who decrees our fate but one who has created each of us as a creature of worth, and who loves us . . . In this world, heroism is not called for; it's enough that we be grateful and make good use of the life that's given us.[37]

35. Yerushalmi, *Freud's Moses*, 95.

36. Freud and Breuer, *Studies on Hysteria*, 306.

37. Kaplan and Schwartz, *Psychology of Hope*, xiii.

Bibliography

PRINTED WORKS

Abraham, Karl. *Selected Papers.* Translated by Douglas Bryan and Alix Strachey. London: Hogart Press & the Institute of Psychoanalysis, 1942.

Aeschines. *The Speeches of Aeschines.* Translated by C. B. Adams. London: Heinemann, 1919.

Alter, Robert. *The David Story.* New York and London: Norton, 1999.

Apollodorus. *Gods and Heroes of the Greeks: The Library of Apollodorus.* Translated and edited by Michael Simpson. Amherst: University of Massachusetts Press, 1976

Aristotle. *The Ethics of Aristotle: The Nichomachean Ethics.* Translated by J. A. K. Thomson. New York: Penguin, 1976.

Bergson, Henri. *Time and Free Will: An Essay on the Immediate Data of Consciousness.* Mineola, NY: Dover Publications, 2001.

Berman, Saul. "Jewish environmental values: The dynamic tension between nature and human needs." *Human Values and the Environment*, volume 140 of IES Report, University of Wisconsin, Madison, 1992.

Bettelheim, Bruno. *Symbolic Wounds.* London: Thames & Hudson, 1955.

Blumenkrantz, Avrohom. *The Laws of Nidah: A Digest.* Far Rockaway, NY: n.p., 1969.

Boman, Thorleif. *Hebrew Thought Compared with Greek.* Translated by Jules L. Moreau. Philadelphia: Westminster, 1960.

Buber, Martin. *The Hebrew Humanism of Martin Buber.* Translated by Noah J. Jacobs. Detroit: Wayne State University Press, 1973.

——. *Israel and the World: Essays in a Time of Crisis.* New York: Shocken, 1963.

Buchler, Adolf. *Types of Jewish-Palestinian Piety from 70 B.C.E. to 70 C.E.: The Ancient Pious Men.* New York: Ktav, 1968.

Camus, Albert. *The Myth of Sisyphus and Other Essays.* Translated by Justin O'Brien. New York: Knopf, 1955.

——. *The Rebel: An Essay on Man in Revolt.* Translated by Anthony Bower. New York: Vintage, 1956.

Cantz, Paul, and Kalman J. Kaplan. "Cross-cultural reflections on the feminine 'other': Hebraism and Hellenism redux." *Pastoral Psychology*, in press.

Cicero, *De Finibus Bonorum et Malorum.* Translated by H. Rackham. New York: Macmillan, 1914.

——. *Tusculan Disputations.* Translated by E. King. Cambridge: Harvard University Press, 1945.

Bibliography

Conon. *Narrationes Quinquaginta et Parthenii Narrationes Amatoriae*. Gottingen: Dietrich, 1798.

Diogenes Laertius. *Lives of Eminent Philosophers*. Translated by Robert D. Hicks. Cambridge: Harvard University Press, Loeb Classical Library, 1972.

Dio Chrysostom. *Orations*. Translated by J. W. Cohoon. London: Heinemann, 1932.

Droge, Arthur, J., and James D. Tabor. *A Noble Death: Suicide and Martyrdom among Christians and Jews in Antiquity*. New York: HarperCollins, 1992.

Durkheim, Emile. *Suicide*. Translated by John. A. Spaulding and George Simpson. Glencoe, IL. : Free Press, 1951.

Eisenstein, Judah D. "Alpha Beta Ben Sira." In *Otsar Midrashim*, vol. 1. Tel Aviv: s.n., 1915.

Epictetus. *The Discourses of Epictetus: With the Enchiridion and Fragments*. Translated by George Long. London: Bell & Sons, 1885.

Erikson, Erik. *Identity, Youth and Crisis*. New York: Norton, 1968.

Exline, Julie J., et al. "Anger, exit, and assertion: Do people see protest toward God as morally acceptable?" *Psychology of Religion and Spirituality*. Advance online publication. doi: 10.1037/a0027667.

Faber, Milton D. *Suicide and Greek Tragedy*. New York: Sphinx, 1970.

Faulkner, William. *Absalom, Absalom!* New York: Random House, 1936.

Fedden, Henry Romilly. *Suicide: A Social and Historical Study*. London: Peter Davies, 1938.

Finley, Moses I. *The World of Odysseus*. New York: Meridian, 1959.

Freud, Sigmund. *Civilization and its Discontents*. In *Standard Edition of the Complete Works of Sigmund Freud*, translated and edited by James Strachey, 21:59–145. London: The Hogart Press & the Institute of Psychoanalysis, 1930.

———. "The Dissolution of the Oedipus Complex." In *Standard Edition of the Complete Works of Sigmund Freud*, translated and edited by James Strachey, 19:173–79. London: Hogart Press & the Institute of Psychoanalysis, 1924.

———. *The Ego and the Id*. In *Standard Edition of the Complete Works of Sigmund Freud*, translated and edited by James Strachey, 19:3–66. London: Hogart Press & the Institute of Psychoanalysis, 1923.

———. "Female Sexuality." In *Standard Edition of the Complete Works of Sigmund Freud*, translated and edited by James Strachey, 21:225–43. London: Hogart Press & the Institute of Psychoanalysis, 1931.

———. *The Future of an Illusion*. In *Standard Edition of the Complete Works of Sigmund Freud*, translated and edited by James Strachey, 21:3–56. London: Hogart Press & the Institute of Psychoanalysis, 1927.

———. "The Infantile Genital Organizations: An interpolation into the theory of sexuality." In *Standard Edition of the Complete Works of Sigmund Freud*, translated and edited by James Strachey, 19:141–45. London: Hogart Press & the Institute of Psychoanalysis, 1923.

———. *The Interpretation of Dreams: Part 1*. In *Standard Edition of the Complete Works of Sigmund Freud*, translated and edited by James Strachey, 5:1–338. London: Hogart Press & the Institute of Psychoanalysis, 1913.

———. *The Interpretation of Dreams: Part 2*. In *Standard Edition of the Complete Works of Sigmund Freud*, translated and edited by James Strachey, 5:339–625. London: Hogart Press & the Institute of Psychoanalysis, 1913.

———. "Some Psychical Consequences of the Anatomical Distinction between the Sexes." In *Standard Edition of the Complete Works of Sigmund Freud*, translated and edited by

James Strachey, 19:241–60. London: Hogart Press & the Institute of Psychoanalysis, 1925.

———. *Totem and Taboo*. In *Standard Edition of the Complete Works of Sigmund Freud*, translated and edited by James Strachey, 13:1–161. London: Hogart Press & the Institute of Psychoanalysis, 1913.

Freud, Sigmund and Joseph Breuer. *Studies in Hysteria*. Translated by Nicola Luckhurst. London: Penguin, 2004.

Friedlander, Ludwig. *Roman Life and Manners: Under the Early Empire*. London: Routledge and Sons, 1928–36.

Gayley, Charles, M. *Classical Myths*. Boston: Atheneum, 1893.

Gouldner, Alvin. *Enter Plato*. New York: Basic, 1965.

Graves, Robert. *The Greek Myths*. Vol. 2. London: Penguin, 1960.

Gray, John. *Men are from Mars, Women are from Venus: A Practical Guide for Improving Communication and Getting What You Want in Your Relationships*. New York: HarperCollins, 1993.

Grotstein, James S. "Why Oedipus and not Christ?: A Psychoanalytic Inquiry into Innocence, Human Sacrifice, and the Sacred-Part I: Innocence, Spirituality, and Human Sacrifice." *The American Journal of Psychoanalysis* 57:3 (1997) 193–220.

———. "Why Oedipus and not Christ?: A Psychoanalytic Inquiry into Innocence, Human Sacrifice, and the Sacred-Part II: The Numinous and Spiritual Dimension as a Metapsychological Perspective." *The American Journal of Psychoanalysis* 57:4 (1997) 317–35.

Hazony, Yoram. *The Philosophy of Hebrew Scriptures*. New York: Cambridge University Press, 2012.

Herodotus. *Histories*. Translated by David Grene. Chicago: University of Chicago Press, 1975.

Hesiod. *The Homeric Hymns and Homerica*. Translated by Hugh G. Evelyn-White. Cambridge: Harvard University Press; London: Heinemann, 1914.

———. *The Works and Days, Theogony, The Shield of Heracles*. Translated by Richmond Lattimore. Ann Arbor: University of Michigan Press, Ann Arbor Paperbacks, 1991.

Holstein, Martha. "Dying Cardinal Bernardin's Way." *Park Ridge Center Bulletin* 1 (1997).

Homer, *The Iliad and The Odyssey*. Translated by Richard Lattimore. Chicago: Encyclopedia Brittanica, 1990.

Hughes, J. Donald. *Pan's Travail: Environmental Problems in Ancient Greece and Rome*. Baltimore: John Hopkins University Press, 1996.

Huizinga, Johan. *Homo Ludens: A Study of the Play Element in Culture*. New York: J. and J. Harper, 1970.

Hyginus, *Hygini Fabulae*. Translated and Edited by Herbert J. Rose. Cambridge: Harvard University Press, Loeb Classical Library, 1934.

Josephus. *Complete Works*. Translated by William Whiston. Grand Rapids: Kregel, 1960.

Jung, Carl G. *The Collected Works*. Volume 4, *Freud and Psychoanalysis*. Translated by R. F. C. Hull. London: Routledge & Kegan Paul, 1961.

Justinian. *The Digest of Justinian*. Translated by A. Watson. Philadelphia: University of Pennsylvania Press, 1985.

Kaplan, Kalman J. "Isaac and Oedipus: An alternative view." *American Journal of Psychoanalysis* 30:4 (2002) 707–17.

———. "Isaac and Oedipus: A reexamination of the father-son relationship." *Judaism* 39 (1990) 73–81.

———. "Obedience and disobedience/rebellion in Biblical versus Greek narratives: Toward a Biblical Psychology." *Pastoral Psychology* 60:5 (2011) 659–70. DOI: 10>1007/s11089-011-0343-x

———. TILT: Teaching Individuals to Live Together. Philadelphia: Brunner/Mazel, 1998.

Kaplan, Kalman J., and Mary Leonhardi. "Kevorkian, Martha Wichorek and us: A personal account." *Omega: Journal of Death and Dying* 40:1 (1999–2000) 231–48.

Kaplan, Kalman J., and Matthew B. Schwartz. *The Seven Habits of the Good Life: How the Biblical Virtues Free Us from the Seven Deadly Sins.* Lanham, MD: Rowman & Littlefield, 2008.

———. *A Psychology of Hope: A Biblical Response to Tragedy and Suicide.* Grand Rapids: Eerdmans, 2008.

Kaplan, Kalman J., et al. *The Family: Biblical and Psychological Foundations.* New York: Human Sciences, 1984.

———. "Individuation and attachment in Israel and Thailand: Secular versus religious Jews and Buddhists." *International Journal of the Psychology of Religion* 22 (2012) 93–105.

Karo, Rabbi Yosef. *Shulchan Aruch*, Jerusalem: Machon Shulchan Melachim, 1560.

Kelman, Herbert C., and V. Lee Hamilton. *Crimes of Obedience: Toward a Social Psychology of Authority and Responsibility.* New Haven: Yale University Press, 1989.

Koenig, Harold. G. *Faith and Mental Health: Religious Resources for Healing.* West Conshohocken, PA: Templeton Foundation Press. 2005

Kohut, Heinz. "Introspection, empathy, and the semi-circle of mental health." *International Journal of Psychoanalysis* 63 (1982) 395–407.

Lafuze, Joan E., et al. "Pastors' perceptions of mental disorders." *Psychiatric Services* 53:7 (2004) 900–901.

Lerner, Melvin J. "Just world research and the attribution process: Looking forward and ahead." *Psychological Bulletin* 85:5 (1978) 1030–51.

Liddell, Henry G., and Robert Scott. *A Greek-English Lexicon.* New York: Oxford University Press, 1996.

Lucian of Samosata. *Lucian.* 8 vols. Translated by A. M. Harmon. London: Heinemann, 1959, 1967.

Maccoby, Hyam. *The Mythmaker: Paul and the Invention of Christianity.* New York: Barnes and Noble, 1986.

Maimonides, Moses. *The Book of Divine Commandments (Sefer HaMitzvot).* London: Soncino, 1940.

———. *Mishne Torah: A Collection of Manuscripts from the Library of the Jewish Theological Seminary.* Ann Arbor: University Microfilms International, 1980

Mann, Thomas. *The Transposed Heads: A Legend of India.* Translated by H. T. Lowe-Porter. New York: Vintage, 1959.

Midrash Rabbah. Edited by H. Freedman and Maurice Simon. Translated by J. Israelstam and Judah Slotkin. 10 vols. London: Soncino, 1939.

Midrash Rabbah. With commentaries of Mattenot Kehuna, Rashi, Messoret Hamidrash, Yefeh To'ar, Perush HaMeharzo. 2 vols. Wilna: 1879. Reprint, New York: E. Grossman, 1953.

Midrash Rabbah. With commentaries of Mattenot Kehuna, Rashi, Messoret Hamidrash, Yefeh To'ar, Perush HaMeharzo. 2 vols. Wilna: 1879. Reprint, New York: E. Grossman, 1953.

Midrash Tanhuma. Translated with introduction, indices and brief notes by John T. Townsend. Hoboken: Ktav, 1989.

Milgram, Stanley. *Obedience to Authority: An Experimental View*. New York: Harper & Row, 1974.

Minuchin, Salvador. *Families and Family Therapy*. Cambridge: Harvard University Press, 1974.

Muzika, E. G." Object relations theory, Buddhism, and the self: Synthesis of eastern and western approaches." *International Philosophical Quarterly* 117 (1990) 59–74.

Oates, Whitney J., and Eugene O'Neill Jr. *The Complete Greek Drama: Volumes 1 and 2*. Translated and edited by Whitney J. Oates and Eugene O'Neill Jr. New York: Random House, 1938.

Ovid. *Fasti*. Translated and edited by Anthony J. Boyle and Roger D. Woodward. London and New York: Penguin, 2000.

———. *The Metamorphoses*. Translated by Charles Boer. Dallas: Spring, 1989.

Plato. "Critias." Translated by A. E. Taylor. In *Plato, The Collected Dialogues, Including the Letters,* edited by Edith Hamilton and Huntington Cairns, 1212–24. Bollingen Series LXXI. Princeton: Princeton University Press, 1999.

———. "Laws." Translated by A. E. Taylor. In *Plato, The Collected Dialogues, Including the Letters,* edited by Edith Hamilton and Huntington Cairns, 1225–1516. Bollingen Series LXXI. Princeton: Princeton University Press, 1999.

———. "Phaedo." Translated by Hugh Tredennick. In *Plato, The Collected Dialogues, Including the Letters,* edited by Edith Hamilton and Huntington Cairns, 40–98. Bollingen Series LXXI. Princeton: Princeton University Press, 1999.

———. "Protagoras" Translated by W. K. C. Guthrie. In *Plato, The Collected Dialogues, Including the Letters,* edited by Edith Hamilton and Huntington Cairns, 308–52. Bollingen Series LXXI. Princeton: Princeton University Press, 1999.

———. "Symposium" Translated by Michael Joyce. In *Plato, The Collected Dialogues, Including the Letters,* edited by Edith Hamilton and Huntington Cairns, 526–74. Bollingen Series LXXI. Princeton: Princeton University Press, 1999.

Pliny the Elder. *The Natural History*. Translated with notes and illustrations by John Bostock and H. T. Riley. London: H. G. Bohn, 1855–57.

Plotinus. *Complete Works*. Translated and edited by Kenneth S. Guthrie. London: Bell & Sons, 1918.

Plutarch. *Morals: Theosophical Essays*. Translated by W. C. King. London: Bell, 1898.

Poe, Edgar. A. "To Helen." In *The Complete Tales and Poems of Edgar Allan Poe*, 1017. New York: Modern Library, 1938.

Quintilian. *Institutiones Oratoriae*. Translated by H. E. Butler. London: Heinemann, 1921–22.

Rank, Otto. *The Double: A Psychoanalytic Study*. Translated and edited with an introduction by Harry Tucker Jr. Chapel Hill: University of North Carolina Press, 1971

Regan, C., et al. "Psychologists and religion: Professional factors and personal beliefs." *Review of Religious Research* 21 (1980) 208–37.

Rolnik, Eran. J. *Freud in Zion: History of Psychoanalysis in Jewish Palestine/Israel 1918–1948*. Tel-Aviv: Am Oved, 2007.

Schwartz, Matthew B., and Kalman J. Kaplan. *Biblical Stories for Psychotherapy and Counseling: A Sourcebook*. Binghamton, NY: Haworth, 2004.

———. *The Fruit of Her Hands: A Psychology of Biblical Woman*. Grand Rapids: Eerdmans, 2007.

Sefer Hachinuch, Author unlisted. Jerusalem: Machon Yerushalayim, 1988

Bibliography

Semonides of Amorgos. In *Greek Lyrics,* translated by Richard Lattimore. Chicago: University of Chicago Press, 1961.

Seneca, Lucius Annaeus. *De Ira (Anger, Mercy, Revenge).* Translated by Robert A. Kaster and Martha C. Nussbaum. Chicago and London: University of Chicago Press, 2010.

———. *Letters from a Stoic: Epistulae Morales ad Lucilium.* Selected and translated with an introduction by Robin Campbell. Harmondsworth, UK: Penguin, 1969.

Shafranske, Edward, and H. Newton Malony. "Clinical psychologists' religious and spiritual orientations and their practice of psychotherapy." *Psychotherapy: Theory, Research, Practice, Training* 27 (1990) 72–8.

Shakespeare, William. *Hamlet.* Cambridge, MA: Houghton Mifflin, 1959.

Shestov, Lev. *Athens and Jerusalem.* Translated by Bernard Martin. New York: Simon and Schuster, 1966.

Shochet, Elijah J. *Animal Life in Jewish Tradition.* New York: Ktav, 1984.

Sifre on Deuteronomy. Edited by Louis Finkelstein. Berlin: Gesellschaft zur Föderung der Wissenschaft des Judentums, 1939. Reprint, New York: Jewish Theological Seminary, 1969.

Simon, Bennett. *Mind and Madness in Ancient Greece: The Classical Roots of Modern Psychiatry.* Ithaca: Cornell University Press, 1978.

Slater, Phillip E. *The Glory of Hera: Greek Mythology and the Greek Family.* Boston: Beacon, 1968.

Snell, Bruno. *The Discovery of the Mind.* New York: Dover, 1982.

Soloveitchik, Joseph. B. "The Lonely Man of Faith." *Tradition* 7:2 (1965) 10–16.

Stephens, William N. *The Oedipus Complex.* New York: Free Press, 1962.

Strabo. *Geographica.* Translated by H. C. Hamilton and W. Falconer. London and New York: Bell & Sons, 1854–57.

Tanakh: The Holy Scriptures. Philadelphia and Jerusalem: Jewish Publication Society, 1985.

Tendler, Moshe D. *Pardes Rimonim: A Marriage Manual for the Jewish Family.* New York: Judaica Press, 1982.

The Oxford Classical Dictionary. Edited by N. G. I. Hammond and H. H. Scullard. 2d ed. Oxford: Clarendon, 1970.

The Pentateuch. Translated and explained by Samson Raphael Hirsch and rendered into English by Isaac Levy. Gateshead: Judaica Press, 1982

The Jerusalem Talmud [Talmud Yerushalmi]. Edited and translated with commentary by Heinrich W. Guggenheimer. Berlin and New York: de Gruyter, 2000.

The New English Bible with the Apocrypha. Oxford: Oxford University Press; Cambridge: Cambridge University Press, 1970.

The Talmud [Talmud Bavli]: The Steinsaltz Edition. Commentary by Adin Steinsaltz. New York: Random House, 1989–99.

Theophrastus. *De Causis Plantarum.* Translated by Benedict Einarson and George K. K. Link. 3 vols. London: Heinemann; Cambridge: Harvard University Press, 1976.

———. *Enquiry into Plants and Minor Works on Odours and Weather Signs.* Translated by Sir Arthur Hoyt. London: Heinemann; New York: Putnam's Sons, 1916.

Twain, Mark. *The Diaries of Adam and Eve.* New York: Oxford University Press, 2010.

Urbach, Ephriam E. *The Sage: Their Concepts and Beliefs.* Translated by I. Abrahms. 2d ed. Jerusalem: Magnes Press of The Hebrew University of Jerusalem, 1979.

Valerius Maximus. *Valeri Maximi Factorum Dictorumque Memorabilium Liborinovem.* London: Valpy, 1823.

Vergil. *The Georgics.* Translated by R. D. Blackmore with an introduction by R. S. Conway and woodcut illustrations by Edward Canick. London: G. W. Jones, 1931.

Veroff, Joseph, et al. *Mental Health in America: Patterns of Help-Seeking from 1957 to 1976.* New York: Basic Books, 1981.

Villiers de l'Isle-Adam, Auguste, Comte de. *Axel.* Translated by June Guicharnaud. New York: Prentice Hall, 1970.

Weaver, Andrew J. "Has there been a failure to prepare and support parish-based clergy in their role as frontline community mental health workers: A review." *Journal of Pastoral Care* 49:2 (1995) 129–47.

Wellisch, Erich. *Isaac and Oedipus: Studies in Biblical Psychology of the Sacrifice of Isaac, The Akedah.* London: Routledge & Kegan Paul, 1954.

White, Kenneth D. *Roman Farming.* Ithaca: Cornell University Press, 1970.

Xenophon. *The Economist.* Translated by Alexander D. O. Wedderburn and W. Gershom Collingwood with a preface by John Ruskin. New York: B. Franklin, 1971.

Yerushalmi, Yosef H. *Freud's Moses. Judaism Terminable and Interminable.* New Haven: Yale University Press, 1991.

FILMS

Anderson, Paul Thomas, director. *There Will Be Blood.* Screenplay adapted loosely from the novel *Oil!* by Sinclair Lewis. A JoAnne Sellar / Ghoulardi Film Company Production. Produced by Paul Thomas Anderson, JoAnne Sellar, and Daniel Lupi. United States: Paramount Vintage, 2007. Film.

Arau, Alfonso, director. *Like Water for Chocolate.* Screenplay by Laura Esquival adapted from novel by Laura Esquival. Spanish with English subtitles. Produced by Arau Films International, Mexican National Council for Culture and the Arts, IMCINE, Mexican Ministry of Tourism and Mexican National Fund for the Development of Tourism. Mexico: Arau Films Inteternacional, 1992. Film.

Burton, Tim, director. *Big Fish.* Screenplay adapted from novel by Daniel Wallace. Produced by Dan Jinks, Bruce Cohen, and Richard D. Zanuck. United States: Columbia Pictures, 2003. Film.

Jones, Tommie Lee, director. *The Sunset Limited.* Screenplay by Cormac McCarthy. Produced for Television by Home Box Office (HBO), the Javelina Film Company, and Professor Productions: United States: Home Box Office, 2011. Television.

Zwick, Edward, director. *Legends of the Fall.* Screenplay by Susan Shilliday and Bill Wittlif adapted from the novella by Jim Harrison. Produced by Bedford-Ralls/Pangaea. United States: TriStar Pictures, 1994. Film.

Subject/Name Index